gluten-free recipes

simple recipes for delicious food every day

rps

RYLAND PETERS & SMALL
LONDON • NEW YORK

Designer Paul Stradling

Commissioning Editor Stephanie Milner

Production Controller David Hearn

Art Director Leslie Harrington

Editorial Director Julia Charles

Publisher Cindy Richards

Indexer Vanessa Bird

First published in 2015 by
Ryland Peters & Small
20–21 Jockey's Fields
London WC1R 4BW
and
341 E 116th St
New York NY 10029

www.rylandpeters.com

Text © Jordan Bourke, Chloe Coker
and Jane Montgomery, Ross Dobson,
Amy Ruth Finegold, Liz Franklin, Tonia
George, Dunja Gulin, Jenny Linford,
Uyen Luu, Hannah Miles, Laura
Washburn and Ryland Peters
& Small 2015

Design and photographs
© Ryland Peters & Small 2015

ISBN: 978-1-84975-597-9

10 9 8 7 6 5 4 3 2 1

A CIP record for this book is available
from the British Library.

US Library of Congress Cataloging-in-
Publication data has been applied for.

Printed and bound in China

notes

• Both British (Metric) and American (Imperial plus US cups)
are included in these recipes for your convenience, however
it is important to work with one set of measurements and not
alternate between the two within a recipe.

• All spoon measurements are level unless otherwise specified.

• All eggs are medium (UK) or large (US), unless specified as
large, in which case US extra-large should be used. Uncooked
or partially cooked eggs should not be served to the very old,
frail, young children, pregnant women or those with
compromised immune systems. Eggs do not contain gluten
and are safe for use following the recipes in this book.

• Ovens should be preheated to the specified temperatures.
We recommend using an oven thermometer. If using a fan-
assisted oven, adjust temperatures according to the
manufacturer's instructions.

• When a recipe calls for the grated zest of citrus fruit, buy
unwaxed fruit and wash well before using. If you can only find
treated fruit, scrub well in warm soapy water before using.

• If you believe that you may have a gluten intolerance or coeliac
disease, it is essential to seek professional medical advice. Once
you have been diagnosed with either, there are many sources of
information available to you. The Coeliac Societies in the UK and
USA are able to provide a large amount of advice and support.

• Disclaimer: The views expressed in this book are general views
only and readers are urged to consult a relevant and qualified
specialist or physician for individual advice before beginning any
dietary regimen. Ryland Peters & Small hereby exclude all liability
to the extent permitted by law for any errors or omissions in this
book and for any loss, damage or expense (whether direct or
indirect) suffered by a third party relying on any information
contained in this book.

gluten-free recipes

contents

introduction

This book provides delicious new ideas for gluten-free recipes plus some alternatives to traditional family favourites that people suffering from coeliac disease, gluten intolerance or wheat allergy may miss the most. Choose from simple breakfast ideas, savoury snacks, tasty quick-fix midweek dishes, comforting baked meals, breads and indulgent cookies, slices and desserts. With a little know-how and some fool-proof recipes, this book will enable you to create delicious free-from food at home that everyone can enjoy.

Some recipes are inherently gluten-free and rely on fresh ingredients and creative seasonings to make them satisfying. Whereas simple substitutions are the key to the success of the baked recipes (both savoury and sweet). Wheat flours are replaced with gluten-free flours, as well as chickpea/gram flour, rice flour, quinoa flour, polenta/cornmeal, tapioca and ground nuts, all of which are readily available. Using ready-blended gluten-free flours lets you bake as you would with regular flour and achieve excellent results. Keep two or three bags in the store-cupboard and you'll be ready to make perfect pastry, breads and cakes whenever needed (see pages 8–11 for detailed information on these and other gluten-free ingredients, as well as how to keep a gluten-free kitchen and manage a gluten-free diet).

The aim of this book is however simple: to enable you to make things that taste so good that you would never know they were gluten-free. You can serve these recipes to the whole family and all of your friends and no one will notice any difference. Free-from has never tasted so good!

What is Coeliac Disease?

Coeliac disease is an auto-immune disease which affects the intestines, leading to poor absorption of gluten. Symptoms of coeliac disease can leave those affected feeling very unwell and lacking in energy, as well as having an upset stomach and other ailments. There is currently no cure for the condition but it can be managed very well by changing to a diet which omits gluten products. It is important that medical advice is taken by anyone who feels they might be experiencing a sensitivity to gluten, to ascertain whether they are a coeliac or are experiencing an allergic reaction to gluten and/or wheat. Each person's symptoms are unique – some people will be able to eat some ingredients that are problematic for others. Testing is available and it is important to take steps to understand what is safe for you to eat. Sometimes coeliac disease is also coupled with other allergies and you may find that some other products, which are gluten-free, also make you unwell. A common example of this is an intolerance to dairy (see the index entry on page 142 for a list of recipes within this book that are also dairy-free).

Managing a Gluten-free Diet

Gluten is present in varying levels in wheat, barley and rye cereals and also sometimes in oats, although this is thought to be most likely caused by cross-contamination with other cereals. Some people sensitive to gluten can eat oats and as these are a good staple ingredient in baking, some of the recipes in this book use them, but always make sure you buy brands labelled 'gluten-free'.

Whilst it is easy to avoid products that obviously contain wheat and gluten – such as bread, cakes or pasta – there are a variety of products that contain traces of gluten, some of which are not obvious. It is not always easy to avoid such pitfalls and it is, therefore, essential to carefully check the ingredients list on product packaging to ensure that a product is gluten-free.

All forms of wheat, barley, rye and spelt must be avoided. This means that regular flours and breads are out, as well as wheat-based products, such as beer and pasta. Gluten is also commonly used by food manufacturers in a wide variety of food preparation processes and can be found in ready-meals and other processed foods. A small trace of wheat used as a thickener in a sauce may make you really unwell, but checking the labelling will help you to spot unsafe ingredients.

Some of the less obvious products that may contain gluten include:

Anti-caking agents – these are used to prevent clumping and sticking together of ingredients during food production and can contain traces of wheat. Anti-caking agents are commonly found in products such as suet but also in icing/confectioners' sugar and dried fruits.

Yeast – some dried yeasts contain wheat as a bulking agent. For safe gluten-free baking, use either fresh yeast or a gluten-free dried yeast.

Baking powder – some baking powders contain wheat. Many manufacturers are now using rice flour in place of wheat flour and so gluten-free baking powder is more commonly available in stores.

Malt products – malted drinks should all be avoided as they are wheat based, but malt extract can usually be tolerated in small amounts, for example in breakfast cereals. Malt vinegar is suitable as the protein is removed in the fermentation process and the traces left are tolerated by the vast majority of coeliacs.

Soy sauce and Worcestershire sauce – these also contain gluten so look out for gluten-free brands. Tamari soy sauce is often gluten-free.

Processed meat products – products such as sausages, sausagemeat, salamis and pâtés can contain traces of wheat, so always read the labels carefully. In recipes which call for sausagemeat, such as the pork sausage rolls on page 32, it can be safest to buy gluten-free sausages and remove the meat from the skins.

Sauces, gravy powders, stocks and powdered spices – these products can sometimes be bulked out with wheat products so, again, always check the labels carefully.

Instant coffees – some contain wheat as a bulking agent. Fresh ground coffee, which can be used to make espresso or filter coffee in a machine can be used instead as these generally do not contain any gluten.

Sour cream – some processes for making sour cream use wheat so it is important to use a brand that is 'pure' and gluten free.

Gluten-free Baking

The key to successful gluten-free cooking is to understand the ingredients and their properties. Gluten gives elasticity to the doughs from which breads and pastries are made. Gluten-free substitutes lack this elasticity and need to be handled slightly differently. Generally speaking, gluten-free doughs and mixes require a lot more liquid than wheat-based recipes and if insufficient liquid is added, the end result can have a powdery texture and crumble when you cut into it. Adding natural yogurt, buttermilk or sour cream can help with this, as will adding cheese or cream cheese and egg yolks to pastry to act as a binding agent.

Pastry can be very crumbly without the elasticity of gluten and must be very carefully worked. Rather than rolling the pastry out into large sheets that are likely to crumble when lifted, the best method for making a pastry case is to gently press small pieces of the pastry dough into the pan until it is lined entirely with a thin layer of pastry. Some gluten-free flours have a slightly bitter taste that can spoil the flavour of baked goods. The best way to mask this is by adding strong flavours.

The Gluten-free Pantry

For successful gluten-free baking you need to equip yourself with a few basic ingredients. Below is a list of essential ingredients you will need for making the recipes from this book.

Gluten-free blended flours – there is now a wide variety of gluten-free flours available in supermarkets and wholefood stores and these are the easiest flours to start with. They are ready mixed and are specifically designed to give the best results. In the UK, four types are available – plain flour which is ideal for pastry and biscuits/cookies, self-raising flour for cakes and some breads, strong white bread flour for breads and some pastries, and strong brown bread flour for bread.
In the US, all-purpose flour is available but not self-rising flour. If you cannot find gluten-free self-raising/rising flour, follow the instructions in each recipe for adding gluten-free baking powder and xanthan gum, which give a very good result. If you are not able to obtain gluten-free bread flour, you can use plain/all-purpose flour and add 1½ teaspoons of xanthan gum to every 125 g/1 cup of flour. You can also combine your own mixes of rice, potato and cornflour/cornstarch in place of these ready-mixed flours.

Gram flour – this is made from ground chickpeas and is often used in Indian cookery. It can be used to make pakora and bhajis as well as various Indian flatbreads. Most poppadoms are made with gram flour, but it is important to check that it has not been combined with wheat flour. Italian farina di ceci is a similar product and can be substituted.

Cornflour/cornstarch – this is made from finely ground grains of corn. It is an excellent thickener for sauces.

Polenta/cornmeal – this is a useful staple of gluten-free baking. Coarse grains can be cooked in water to a thick paste and added to savoury muffins and breads to give a lovely golden colour, moist texture and rich flavour. Fine cornmeal is more like flour in texture and can be used in breads and muffins.

Quinoa flour – this flour is made from ground quinoa grains which are gluten-free, nutritious and have a great texture. It is particularly good for making pasta.

Ondhwa flour – this is an Indian flour made from ground rice and lentils and is available in Indian supermarkets and online.

Oat Flour – this is made from finely ground oats. As stated on page 8, some oats contain traces of gluten so it is important to ensure that the oat flour you use is gluten-free and that the person you are cooking for can eat oats.

Oats – not all people who are intolerant to gluten are able to eat oats. The protein in oats is similar to gluten and so can also be an issue for some coeliacs. If in doubt, do not use them. However, there are many people who are intolerant to gluten who are able to eat oats, but make sure you choose brands labelled 'gluten-free'.

Almond meal and ground almonds – almond meal is a coarse ground flour which contains the skin of the whole almonds. It is therefore darker in texture than ground almonds. Ground almonds are useful in gluten-free baking as they give cakes lots of moisture and do not have a strong flavour so can carry other flavours well. You can make your own ground almonds or almond meal by blitzing whole or skinned almonds in a food processor. When buying ready-ground almonds, check the ingredients as some varieties include breadcrumbs as a bulking agent (and therefore gluten).

Gluten-free baking powder – this is an essential raising agent, which is used to make cakes and breads rise.

Xanthan gum – this is used in gluten-free baking to bind, thicken and stabilize ingredients and is ideal for use in doughs, pastry and breads.

Flavouring agents – flavourings are ideal for masking the sometimes bitter flavour of gluten-free flours. Truffle oil, dried mushrooms, Parmesan cheese, black pepper and mustard are all good agents.

Dairy ingredients – essential in gluten-free baking given the crumbly nature of gluten-free doughs. The recipes in this book use buttermilk, plain yogurt and sour cream.

Butter and fats – some margarines may contain gluten, so it is best to use good-quality unsalted butter in all recipes to remain gluten-free.

Alcohols – this can be a slightly confusing area for those who are gluten-intolerant. Beer is made with hops and so must be avoided. Some brands of whisky (and cream-based whisky liqueurs) may contain gluten from the caramel colouring which is added, although pure whisky does not contain gluten.

Avoiding Contamination

One key requirement of successful gluten-free cooking is to avoid cross-contamination. If you have a member of the family who is intolerant to gluten, the best solution is to remove all products containing gluten from the house. Whilst this is the most effective way to avoid the risk of cross contamination, this is not always practical. Where total removal is not possible, the best advice is to keep gluten-free products in sealed containers in a separate place away from products containing gluten. Label everything clearly so that there can be no confusion as to what is or isn't gluten-free.

If you have been baking with regular flour, small particles will have been released into the air during cooking, which can land on cooking equipment, surfaces and even kitchen towels and leave traces of gluten. It is therefore very important to wipe down all equipment, surfaces and utensils thoroughly and to use clean cloths and aprons. Cross-contamination is also possible through using kitchen appliances and equipment, such as toasters, baking sheets and wire cooling racks. Silicon sleeves (Toastabags) can be used to shield toasters from gluten contamination. Consider investing in silicon mats that you can set aside just for gluten-free baking. If it is practical, keep separate tubs and jars of butters, spreads and preserves clearly labelled as 'gluten-free'.

From wholesome bowls of porridge and indulgent pancakes for when you have time to sit down, to on-the-go energy bars and granola to eat on the move, this chapter offers healthy recipes that make the perfect gluten-free yet energizing start to the day.

breakfasts

porridge

Porridge is nourishing and sustaining so start the day with a bowlful and you won't have any energy crashes mid-morning. While many of us are inclined to add milk, cream and sugar, porridge is the perfect vessel for all manner of superfood ingredients, like the tangy, red goji berries and pumpkin seeds used here.

130 g/1 cup gluten-free jumbo rolled oats

150 ml/²⁄₃ cup dairy, rice, soy or nut milk, plus extra to taste

1 banana, peeled and mashed

25 g/¼ cup fresh or frozen blueberries

25 g/¼ cup (dark) raisins

a pinch of ground cinnamon

2 tablespoons pumpkin seeds

2 tablespoons dried goji berries or cranberries

2–4 tablespoons maple syrup or runny honey

Serves 2

Put the oats in a saucepan or pot and cover with the rice milk and 150 ml/²⁄₃ cup of water. Cook gently over low–medium heat, stirring more and more frequently as the mixture begins to thicken. Oats absorb a huge amount of liquid, so they become thick and gloopy very quickly. Some people love it at this consistency, but if you prefer your porridge a little more runny, then just keep adding more rice milk and water, a little at a time, until you reach the desired consistency. When ready, turn the heat right down to the lowest heat.

Now add the mashed banana, blueberries, raisins, cinnamon, pumpkin seeds, goji berries and the tiniest drop of maple syrup. Stir well to warm each of the ingredients before serving with a little extra maple syrup to taste.

2 bananas, peeled and mashed

3 tablespoons coconut oil, melted

grated zest of 1 lemon, plus 1 tablespoon freshly squeezed lemon juice

15 dried apricots, diced

1 teaspoon rum (optional)

200 g/2¼ cups millet flakes (or gluten-free steel-cut oats)

¼ teaspoon ground cinnamon

⅛ teaspoon bourbon vanilla powder or vanilla extract

3 tablespoons unsweetened cocoa powder (ideally raw)

a pinch of salt

a 18-cm/7-in. square baking dish, lined with clingfilm/plastic wrap

Makes 8 bars

These bars are amazing for breakfast or as a pick-me-up anytime snack. You can use any other dried fruits instead of the apricots, or try adding orange zest and juice instead of lemon for a delicious chocolate-orange flavoured bar.

pure energy bars

Put the mashed bananas in a large mixing bowl and pour over the coconut oil. Add the lemon zest and juice, the apricots and rum, if using. Stir well and set aside.

In a separate large mixing bowl, combine the millet flakes, cinnamon, vanilla, cocoa and salt. Add the banana mixture to the dry ingredients and use a spatula to combine the ingredients really well – there should be no dry patches of oats and the dough should be thick and sticky.

Place the dough in the prepared baking dish and use a spatula or your hands to press down the mixture until you get an even layer about 1½ cm/½ in. thick. Cover with clingfilm/plastic wrap and chill in the fridge for at least 2 hours, or overnight.

Unwrap the dough and cut into 8 even bars. Serve immediately or wrap each one individually and enjoy throughout the week!

125 g/½ cup maple syrup

125 g/½ cup clear honey

4 tablespoons sunflower oil

250 g/2 cups gluten-free rolled oats

75 g/⅔ cup shelled almonds, roughly chopped

75 g/⅔ cup shelled Brazil nuts, roughly chopped

50 g/⅓ cup pumpkin seeds

½ teaspoon salt

100 g/⅔ cup sultanas/golden raisins

1–2 large baking sheets, greased and lined with baking parchment

Serves 10–12

Mmmm, crunchy honeyed granola. This version is very sweet and crunchy, and quite rich, so you don't need a lot. Try adding a scattering to a bowl of plain yogurt. The trick is to get the granola to brown evenly, so you need it to be spread out evenly and to turn it during roasting. Don't let it become too dark or it can get bitter. If in doubt, remove from the oven and let it cool a little, taste it and put it back in for longer if necessary.

nutty honey granola

Preheat the oven to 140°C (275°F) Gas 1.

Put the maple syrup, honey and oil in a small saucepan or pot and set over low heat to warm through.

Put the oats, nuts, seeds and salt in a large mixing bowl and stir well. Pour over the warmed syrup and mix thoroughly with a wooden spoon. All the oats must be moistened.

Spread the mixture over the prepared baking sheets, making sure it is no deeper than 1 cm/½ in., and bake in the preheated oven for 20 minutes.

Remove the sheets from the oven and stir the toasted, golden granola from the edges to the middle, then smooth out again. Return to the oven for a further 15–20 minutes, until lightly golden. Don't expect it to become crunchy – the mixture will remain soft until it cools.

Remove from the oven and let cool for 10 minutes before stirring in the raisins. Let cool completely, then break into pieces. Store in an airtight container and eat within 1 month.

breakfast muffins

4–6 smoked streaky bacon rashers/strips, cooked and broken into small strips

60 g/4 tablespoons butter, softened

1 tablespoon caster/granulated sugar

1 large egg, plus 6 small eggs

45 g/⅓ cup gluten-free self-raising/rising flour (or 45 g/⅓ cup gluten-free all-purpose flour plus ½ teaspoon baking powder and ¼ teaspoon xanthan gum)

15 g/2 tablespoons ground almonds

15 g/2 tablespoons fine cornmeal

1 tablespoon crème fraîche or sour cream

6 cherry vine tomatoes, halved

salt and ground black pepper

a 6-hole large muffin pan lined with 6 high-sided muffin cases

Makes 6

These satisfying muffins encapsulate the main elements of a classic English fried breakfast, with bacon, tomatoes and even a whole egg on top. They are best served straight from the oven while still warm. Use high-sided muffin cases, which can hold a whole egg, and don't overfill with the muffin mixture, otherwise your eggs will spill over.

Preheat the oven to 180°C (350°F) Gas 4.

Reserve 6 small strips of bacon to decorate the muffins and blitz the remaining bacon to fine crumbs in a food processor.

In a large mixing bowl, whisk together the butter, sugar, large egg and the bacon crumbs. Add the flour (plus baking powder and xanthan gum, if using), almonds, cornmeal and crème fraîche and whisk well so that everything is incorporated. Season well with salt and pepper.

Place a large spoonful of the batter into each of the muffin cases in the prepared pan and top each with 2 tomato halves, then cover the tomatoes with another spoonful of batter. Carefully crack one of the small eggs into a bowl, then pour it onto the top of one of the muffins, taking care that it doesn't spill over the edge of the case (hold back a little of the egg white if the case is close to overflowing). Repeat with the remaining 5 small eggs and muffins. Sprinkle a little black pepper over each egg and lay one of the reserved bacon strips on top of each muffin. Bake in the preheated oven for 15–20 minutes.

Remove from the oven and serve straight away.

pancakes with fried bananas

100 g/¾ cup gluten-free plain/all-purpose flour (or 50 g/6 tablespoons rice flour plus 30 g/¼ cup tapioca flour and 25 g/3 tablespoons gram/chickpea flour)

½ teaspoon baking powder

a pinch of salt

2 eggs

200 ml/¾ cup dairy or rice milk

sunflower oil, to fry

Fried bananas

2 bananas, peeled and sliced

freshly squeezed juice of 1 orange

2 teaspoons maple syrup, runny honey or agave syrup

1 teaspoon ground cinnamon

1 teaspoon desiccated/shredded coconut, plus extra to serve

Makes about 5

It is just as easy to make delicious wheat-free pancakes as it is regular American or French versions.

Begin by preparing the pancake batter. Sift the flour (or flours), baking powder and salt into a large mixing bowl and make a well in the middle. In a separate bowl, whisk together the eggs and milk. Gradually pour the egg mixture into the well in the flour mixture, mixing all the time until you get a smooth batter. Cover with clingfilm/plastic wrap and set aside to allow the batter to rest for at least 30 minutes, or overnight in the fridge.

To make the fried bananas, heat a little oil in a separate large non-stick frying pan/skillet set over a high heat. Add the sliced bananas to the pan and sauté until golden. Add the orange juice, honey, cinnamon and coconut. Let the liquid bubble away for 30 seconds, then remove from the heat and transfer to a bowl.

When ready, heat a little oil in a non-stick frying pan/skillet until hot. Stir the batter and pour a small ladleful into the pan, swirling so that the mixture spreads to the edges. Cook for 1 minute, until the top of the pancake starts to bubble, then flip it over and cook until golden. Keep the pancakes warm while you cook the remaining batter.

Add some of the fried bananas to each pancake, fold in half and then in half again. Sprinkle over a little more coconut and serve immediately with a little of the honey from the fried bananas.

The raising agent in crumpets is yeast, and when the batter is exposed to the heat of the frying pan/skillet, the air created by the yeast during its 'proving' expands and rises to the top of the crumpet, so they develop little holes on top. These are densely textured crumpets so don't worry if the batter looks uncooked, as they are toasted before serving. You could buy specially-made crumpet rings, but they can be hard to find. Egg cooking rings do the job nicely but must be well greased before they are filled with batter.

semolina crumpets

125 g/1 cup gluten-free strong white bread flour

125 g/1 cup fine semolina

1 teaspoon golden caster/natural cane sugar

1 tablespoon dried yeast

50 g/½ stick unsalted butter

To serve

fruit jam/jelly

whipped cream

butter and honey (optional)

a high-speed blender

4 crumpet or egg cooking rings, each about 8–10 cm/3–4 in. diameter, well greased

Makes 8–10 crumpets

Put the flour, semolina, sugar and yeast into a blender. With the motor running, slowly add 325 ml/1⅓ cups warm water and continue to blend for 1 minute more. Scrape down the sides of the blender and blend for a further 30 seconds so the mixture is free of lumps.

Pour the batter into a large bowl, cover with clingfilm/plastic wrap and set in a warm place for 45–60 minutes, until the mixture is very frothy and bubbly.

Generously grease a heavy-based frying pan/skillet with butter and set over high heat. Sit the prepared cooking rings in the pan. Stir the rested batter once and ladle about 125 ml/½ cup into each ring. Cook for 4–5 minutes, until bubbles form on the top and the sticky dough has dried on the top. Do not turn over. Transfer the cooked crumpets to a wire rack to cool and continue to cook the crumpets in batches until all the batter has been used, regreasing the pan each time.

Lightly toast the tops of the crumpets in an electric toaster or under a grill/broiler on high, until golden. Serve hot with fruit jam/jelly and whipped cream, or butter and honey, as preferred.

caramelized chicory with Black Forest ham and poached eggs

25 g/2 tablespoons butter

4 chicory/endive heads, halved lengthways

4 eggs

100 g/2 cups rocket/arugula

8 slices Black Forest ham

25 g/⅓ cup shaved Parmesan

salt and ground black pepper

Dressing

1 garlic clove, peeled and finely chopped

1 red chilli/chile, finely chopped

1 tablespoon red wine vinegar

2 tablespoons extra virgin olive oil

grated zest and freshly squeezed juice of ½ lemon

Serves 4

Chicory/endive is such an underrated vegetable. It is very different when cooked, becoming silky smooth and slightly bitter, which is why it works so well against a sweet, smoky ham like Black Forest ham. The chilli/chile and lemon in the dressing wake up all the flavours.

Preheat the oven to 150°C (300°F) Gas 2.

To make the dressing, put the garlic, chilli/chile and vinegar in a mixing bowl and whisk in the olive oil and lemon zest and juice.

Heat the butter in a large frying pan/skillet set over a low heat and add the chicory/endive, cut side down. Season with salt and pepper, cover with a lid and cook gently for 5–6 minutes. Remove the lid, turn up the heat and continue to cook for 5 minutes, until the chicory/endive is golden. Turn the chicory/endive halves over and cook for 3–4 minutes, until the outer leaves begin to caramelize. Keep warm in the preheated oven.

Fill a large, deep frying pan/skillet with water and bring to a simmer over a medium heat. Crack the eggs into the water, and poach for exactly 3 minutes. Remove the eggs from the pan with a slotted spoon and drain on paper towels.

To serve, place a mound of rocket/arugula on each plate, top with 2 chicory/endive halves and drape over the Black Forest ham. Place a poached egg on each plate and scatter over some Parmesan shavings. Finish with a drizzle of dressing and enjoy.

You won't go hungry with these ideas for delicious gluten-free snacks. Bake pastry classics such as sausage rolls, or try finger-licking sweet and spicy spareribs, buttermilk fried chicken and smoked haddock mini Scotch eggs.

savoury snacks

Italian puff canapés

These small flaky pastry bites make a delicious hot snack, topped with tomatoes, mozzarella and fresh basil.

200 g/1 stick plus 5 tablespoons butter, grated and chilled

175 g/1⅓ cups gluten-free plain/all-purpose flour, sifted, plus extra for dusting

2 teaspoons freshly squeezed lemon juice

1 teaspoon xanthan gum

60–80 ml/¼–⅓ cup ice-cold water

To assemble

5–6 tablespoons green pesto

16 cherry tomatoes, halved

32 mozzarella pearls

salt and ground black pepper, to season

leaves from a bunch of fresh basil

extra virgin olive oil, for drizzling

a stand mixer (optional)

8-cm/3½-in. and 6-cm/2½-in. round cookie cutters

a large baking sheet, greased and lined with baking parchment

Makes 16

Rub half of the grated butter into the flour using your fingertips. Add the lemon juice and xanthan gum. Cut in the cold water, a little at a time, using a round-bladed knife, until you have a soft but not sticky dough. Roll out the pastry on a lightly floured surface to a large rectangle. Sprinkle half of the remaining grated butter over the pastry and dust liberally with flour. Fold the bottom third of the rectangle into the middle. Press the folded pastry down with your hands before taking the top third of the pastry and folding it down over the top. Press down again with your hands. Turn the pastry over and roll out into a large rectangle again. Sprinkle with the remaining grated butter, dust again with flour and repeat the folding steps. Repeat the rolling-out stages twice more.

Preheat the oven to 180°C (350°F) Gas 4.

Roll out the pastry to a rectangle 2–3 mm/⅛ in. thick. Stamp out 16 rounds with the large cookie cutter and transfer to the prepared baking sheet. Using the small cutter, imprint a circle into centre of each round. Spoon a little pesto into the middle, then place 2 tomato halves on top with 2 mozzarella pearls. Season well.

Bake in the preheated oven for 10–15 minutes, until golden brown. Sprinkle with basil and drizzle with a little oil to serve.

80 g/5 tablespoons butter, diced and chilled

180 g/1⅓ cups gluten-free plain/all-purpose flour, sifted, plus extra for dusting

1 teaspoon gluten-free Dijon mustard

1 tablespoon cream cheese

1 egg yolk

Filling

1 small onion, finely diced

1 tablespoon olive oil

400 g/14 oz. gluten-free pork sausagemeat (or 8 gluten-free pork sausages, skin removed)

1 small apple, peeled, cored and grated

salt and ground black pepper

Glaze

1 egg, beaten

2 teaspoons Dijon mustard

a baking sheet, greased and lined with baking parchment

Makes 12

Who doesn't love a good sausage roll? In this recipe, the grated apple keeps the meat moist. Sausagemeat is readily available, but it often contains gluten, so check the packaging or use gluten-free sausages, removing the skins before using.

pork sausage rolls

For the pastry, rub the butter into the flour with your fingertips. Add the mustard, cream cheese and egg yolk and mix together to form a soft dough, adding a little water if the mixture is too dry. Bring the dough together into a ball, wrap in clingfilm/plastic wrap and chill in the fridge for at least 1 hour.

To prepare the filling, cook the onion in the olive oil until soft and translucent, then set aside to cool. In a separate bowl, mix the sausagemeat and grated apple together. Add the cooked onion, mix and season well. Cover and chill in the fridge.

Preheat the oven to 180°C (350°F) Gas 4.

Remove the pastry from the fridge and divide it into two portions. Roll out each portion on a lightly floured surface to a rectangle measuring about 30 x 18 cm/12 x 7 in. Shape half of the sausage mixture into a long roll. Take one of the pastry rectangles and place the sausage roll down the centre of the long length. Wet both long edges of the rectangle with a little water and fold one of the halves over the sausage mixture so that it meets the pastry edge on the other side. Press down with your fingertips to seal in the sausagemeat and crimp the edges. Trim away any excess pastry and cut the slice into 6 sausage rolls. Repeat with the remaining pastry and sausage mixture. Transfer to the prepared baking sheet. Whisk together the egg and mustard and brush over the tops of the sausage rolls. Sprinkle with a little black pepper and bake in the preheated oven for 25–30 minutes until the pastry is golden brown and the sausagemeat is cooked.

Cheese and crackers served with a tangy chutney make a great no-hassle snack any time of the day. These crackers, bursting with Cheddar cheese, are rich and buttery, and melt in the mouth. They are quick and easy to prepare and will keep well in an airtight container, although they are quite fragile, so store them carefully.

cheese crackers

170 g/1⅓ cups gluten-free plain/all-purpose flour, plus extra for dusting

115 g/1 stick butter, diced and chilled

100 g/1 cup grated Cheddar cheese

milk, to loosen (optional)

a 7½-cm/3-in. round cookie cutter

a large baking sheet, greased and lined with baking parchment

Makes 15

Preheat the oven to 180°C (350°F) Gas 4.

Sift the flour into a large mixing bowl. Rub the butter into the flour with your fingertips until it resembles fine breadcrumbs. Add the cheese and mix together to form a soft dough, adding a little water or milk if the mixture is too dry. Wrap the dough in clingfilm/plastic wrap and chill in the fridge for at least 1 hour.

Roll out the dough on a lightly floured surface to about 2–3 mm/⅛ in. thick and stamp out 15 rounds with the cookie cutter. Arrange the crackers on the prepared baking sheet and bake in the preheated oven for 10–15 minutes until golden brown. Leave to cool on the baking sheet before serving.

sweet and spicy spareribs

4 Asian shallots, peeled and finely chopped

1 large garlic clove, peeled and finely chopped

4 teaspoons English mustard

4 teaspoons gluten-free soy sauce

6 tablespoons gluten-free hoisin sauce

1 tablespoon Sriracha chilli/hot pepper sauce

1 teaspoon clear honey

800 g/1¾ lbs. pork spareribs

1 teaspoon sesame seeds (optional)

Serves 4–6

This mouthwatering recipe includes English mustard, an ingredient that makes these spareribs completely addictive. The combination of Asian flavours offers a delightful alternative to traditional store-bought barbecue sauce (which often contains gluten) on these pork ribs.

In a bowl, mix together all the ingredients except the spareribs and sesame seeds to make a marinade. Add the ribs and rub the marinade in well. Cover and refrigerate for at least 30 minutes.

Preheat the oven to 200°C (400°F) Gas 6.

Transfer the ribs to a roasting pan and roast in the preheated oven for 45 minutes or until cooked through and the juices run clear when you stick a knife in. The meat can also be grilled on a barbecue, in which case times will vary, so check that it's cooked through before serving.

Scatter the sesame seeds over the top before serving, if using.

225 g/1½ cups plus 1 tablespoon gluten-free plain/all-purpose flour

1½ teaspoons baking powder

½ teaspoon salt

30 g/2 tablespoons butter

225 ml/1 cup milk

1 egg, lightly beaten

160 g/1 heaped cup canned or frozen sweetcorn

½–1 fresh red chilli/chile, finely chopped (or 1 teaspoon chilli/hot red pepper flakes)

a small handful of fresh coriander/cilantro, finely chopped, plus leaves, to serve

crème fraîche/sour cream, to serve

Spicy avocado salsa

2 avocados, pitted/stoned

2 tablespoons freshly chopped coriander/cilantro, plus a few leaves to garnish

2 small shallots, peeled and finely chopped

1–2 red chillies/chiles, finely chopped

grated zest of 2 limes, plus 2 tablespoons freshly squeezed juice

a pinch of sugar

salt and ground black pepper

Makes 24

corncakes with spicy avocado salsa

These light, fresh-tasting corncakes are ideal served as a light snack with drinks. They also make a great brunch dish – simply make the corncakes slightly bigger (a tablespoon of batter makes a 6-cm/2½-in. wide pancake), layer with the salsa and serve with a dollop of sour cream.

To make the spicy avocado salsa, half chop, half mash the avocado (depending on its ripeness) and combine with the coriander/cilantro and shallots in a bowl, then add the remaining ingredients. Season well with salt and pepper. Taste and adjust the seasoning as required using more lime juice, chilli/chile or sugar, if needed.

For the corncakes, sift the flour into a large mixing bowl and add the baking powder and salt. Set aside.

Melt the butter in a small saucepan or pot set over low heat. In a separate bowl combine the milk, egg, sweetcorn, chilli/chile and coriander/cilantro. Add the melted butter and stir to combine.

Make a well in the centre of the dry ingredients. Pour in the wet ingredients and stir from the centre to gradually mix them together so that there are no lumps. Set aside for 10 minutes.

Lightly grease a frying pan/skillet and let it heat up over a medium-high heat. Put teaspoons of the mixture into the pan (it will spread a little). Cook until the pancakes are golden brown, turning over halfway through.

To serve, top with a spoonful of spicy avocado salsa, a little crème fraîche and a coriander/cilantro leaf.

250 g/3 cups grated courgette/zucchini

4 spring onions/scallions, finely sliced

grated zest and freshly squeezed juice of 1 lemon

1 teaspoon vegetable oil, plus extra for deep-frying

3 tablespoons gram/chickpea flour

1 teaspoon baking powder

salt and ground black pepper

Minted yogurt

½ cucumber, deseeded and grated

200 g/1 cup thick plain yogurt

½ garlic clove, peeled and crushed

a handful of freshly chopped mint

a squeeze of fresh lemon juice

½ teaspoon sugar

Serves 4

These fritters are perfect for enjoying with drinks. You can use any vegetable you like and carrots, beetroot or onions all work well. Try adding feta, herbs, spices and chilli/chile for extra flavour – just experiment with whatever you find in your fridge.

courgette fritters with minted yogurt

To make the minted yogurt dip, put the grated cucumber in a sieve/strainer set over a bowl and leave for 10 minutes to drain any excess liquid. Put the drained grated cucumber in a bowl with the yogurt. Add and stir in the crushed garlic and the chopped mint. Add a squeeze of lemon juice and the sugar. Season well.

To make the fritters, sprinkle the courgette/zucchini with salt and put it in a strainer set over a bowl for 10 minutes to draw out any moisture. Alternatively, you can squeeze out any liquid in a clean kitchen towel.

Put the drained grated courgette/zucchini in a bowl, add the spring onions/scallions, lemon zest and juice and teaspoon of vegetable oil, and stir till thoroughly mixed. Combine the gram/chickpea flour and baking powder, sprinkle them over the vegetables, then stir until well combined.

These fritters are best made in a deep-fat fryer. If you don't have a deep-fat fryer, put about 2 cm/¾ in. of oil in the bottom of a wok. Heat the oil until it is hot but not smoking. Drop teaspoons of mixture into the oil and cook for about 2 minutes until they are crisp and golden.

Remove the fritters with a slotted spoon and drain on paper towels. Sprinkle the fritters with salt while they are still hot. The fritters are best served immediately but will keep for a short time in a warm oven.

130 g/1 cup pumpkin seeds

130 g/1 cup sunflower seeds

50 g/½ cup walnuts

5 tablespoons freshly chopped flat-leaf parsley

5 dried tomato halves, soaked and finely diced

2 garlic cloves, peeled and crushed

3 tablespoons olive oil

freshly squeezed juice of ½ lemon

1 teaspoon dried oregano

salt and ground black pepper, to taste

Makes 24

Here's a no-cook chickpea-free falafel that's surprisingly easy to make. It's a great lunchbox filler and the mixture will stay fresh in the fridge for several days. These falafel go with just about anything – in salads, with cooked vegetables, alongside soups or as an appetizer. It's a great way to introduce more seeds into your diet!

seed falafel

Grind the seeds in a food processor into a fine flour, making sure you don't process them for too long, otherwise they might turn into seed butter. Finely chop the walnuts, as they'll give the falafels a nice crunchy texture. Add them, together with the remaining ingredients, to the seed flour and mix well with your hands or with a silicone spatula. Taste and adjust the seasoning if necessary – it should taste strong and full of flavour. Try squeezing the seed mixture in your hand and if it doesn't fall apart it's moist enough. In case it feels dry and crumbles immediately, add 1 tablespoon of water and mix again.

Form the mixture into walnut-sized falafel balls and either serve straight away or keep in the fridge for up to 3 days.

buttermilk fried chicken

2 garlic cloves, crushed

1 thumb-sized piece of fresh ginger, peeled and crushed

½ teaspoon chilli powder

1 teaspoon freshly chopped fresh thyme leaves

300 ml/1¼ cups buttermilk

salt and ground black pepper

8 chicken drumsticks

200 g/1½ cups gluten-free plain/all-purpose flour

1 teaspoon ground ginger

sunflower oil, for deep-frying

coleslaw, to serve

Serves 4

Making a marinade with buttermilk to coat drumsticks before frying them makes for tender, flavourful chicken. This is a thoroughly tasty dish, and will become a family favourite. Serve with crunchy coleslaw on the side.

Put the garlic, ginger, chilli powder, thyme and buttermilk in a large mixing bowl and stir well to make the marinade. Season with salt and pepper.

Add the chicken drumsticks to the marinade and coat well. Cover and chill in the fridge for at least 8 hours or overnight.

In a shallow bowl, mix together the flour and ground ginger and season with salt and pepper.

Shake any excess marinade from the chicken drumsticks and coat them thoroughly in the seasoned flour.

Pour the oil into a large, deep frying pan/skillet to around 2 cm/¾ in. depth and set over a high heat. Allow the oil to become very hot. Test that the pan is the right heat by dropping in a small piece of bread; if it turns brown very quickly, the oil is hot enough.

Add the chicken drumsticks to the pan, cooking them in batches if the pan isn't large enough for them all, and fry for around 15–20 minutes, until they are a rich golden-brown on all sides. Remove the chicken drumsticks from the pan, drain on paper towels and serve immediately with coleslaw.

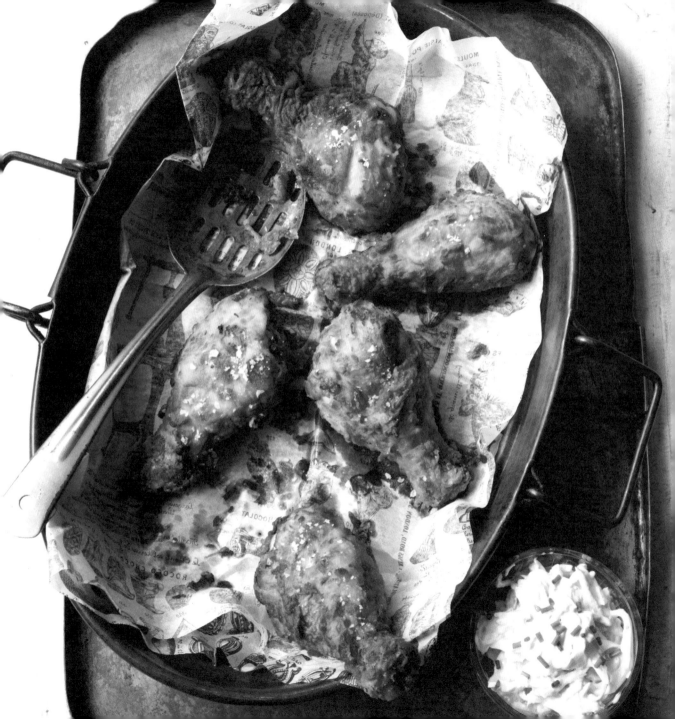

tomato, basil and feta muffins

350 g/2¾ cups gluten-free self-raising/rising flour plus 1 teaspoon baking powder (or 350 g/2¾ cups gluten-free plain/all-purpose flour, plus 4 teaspoons baking powder and 2 teaspoons xanthan gum)

1 teaspoon bicarbonate of/baking soda

250 ml/1 cup milk

250 ml/1 cup plain yogurt

2 eggs

100 g/6½ tablespoons butter, melted and cooled

2 tablespoons tomato purée/paste

160 g/¾ cup (drained weight) sundried tomatoes preserved in oil, chopped, plus 1 tablespoon of the oil

200 g/7 oz. feta cheese, diced

3 tablespoons freshly chopped basil leaves

salt and ground black pepper

3 x 6-hole muffin pans lined with 16 muffin cases

Makes 16

These muffins make a delicious savoury snack, are great served as a side to soup or a salad, or packed for a picnic lunch. The addition of feta cheese adds a lovely fresh and tangy flavour and gives them a moist texture.

Preheat the oven to 180°C (350°F) Gas 4.

Sift the flour, baking powder (plus xanthan gum, if using) and bicarbonate of/baking soda into a large mixing bowl.

In a separate bowl, whisk together the milk, yogurt, eggs, melted butter and tomato purée/paste, then add this to the flour mixture. Whisk everything together well and season with salt and pepper. Mix the tomatoes and feta cheese into the mixture, along with the tomato oil and chopped basil.

Divide the mixture between the muffin cases, making sure that some of the pieces of cheese and sundried tomato sit on the top of each muffin. Bake the muffins in the preheated oven for 20–30 minutes until golden brown. Serve warm or cold.

The muffins will keep for up to 2 days in an airtight container, but can be frozen and then reheated to serve.

350 g/2¾ cups gluten-free self-raising/rising flour plus 2 teaspoons baking powder (or 350 g/2¾ cups gluten-free plain/all-purpose flour, plus 5 teaspoons baking powder and 2 teaspoons xanthan gum), plus extra flour for dusting

100 g/⅔ cup ground almonds

115 g/1 stick butter, chilled and cubed

70 g/⅓ cup mascarpone cheese

20 g/⅓ cup grated Parmesan cheese

120 g/1 generous cup grated Cheddar cheese

120 g/1 generous cup grated red Leicester cheese (or other hard cheese)

200–250 ml/¾–1 cup milk, plus extra to glaze

ground black pepper

a 7½-cm/3-in. round fluted cookie cutter

a baking sheet, greased and lined with baking parchment

Makes 10

A cheese scone, served warm from the oven and spread with butter, is one of life's simple pleasures. These scones contain four different types of cheese – salty Parmesan, creamy mascarpone, tangy Cheddar and golden red Leicester.

four-cheese scones

Preheat the oven to 180°C (350°F) Gas 4.

Sift the flour and baking powder (plus xanthan gum, if using) into a large mixing bowl, add the ground almonds and butter and rub in the butter with your fingertips until the mixture resembles fine breadcrumbs. Mix in the mascarpone cheese, then fold in the Parmesan and two-thirds of the Cheddar and red Leicester cheeses, reserving a third of each to top the scones. Gradually add the milk and bring together into a soft dough, adding a little more milk if needed.

Roll out the dough on a lightly floured surface to about 2½ cm/ 1 in. thick and stamp out the scones using the cookie cutter, re-rolling the trimmings as necessary. You should only re-roll the dough once, as it will become crumbly with the extra flour and difficult to roll.

Lay the scones on the prepared baking sheet, spacing them well apart. Use a pastry brush to brush the tops with a little extra milk, sprinkle over the remaining cheese and top with a little pepper.

Bake in the preheated oven for 20–25 minutes until the tops are golden and the scones sound hollow when you tap them. Serve warm or cold.

The scones do not keep well and so are best eaten on the day they are made, or they can be frozen and reheated to serve.

8 quails' eggs (or 4 small hen's eggs)

500 ml/2 cups milk

1 garlic clove, peeled and thinly sliced

150 g/5½ oz. potatoes, peeled and quartered

1 sprig of fresh thyme

250 g/9 oz. undyed smoked haddock, deboned

4 slices gluten-free bread (see pages 126–141), blended to a fine crumb (or store-bought gluten-free breadcrumbs)

3–4 tablespoons gluten-free plain/all-purpose flour

2 eggs, beaten

vegetable oil, for frying

salt and ground black pepper

Makes 8 mini or 4 standard

Rather than the traditional sausagemeat, these cute little quails' eggs are wrapped in a smoked haddock mixture, then coated in crispy gluten-free breadcrumbs.

smoked haddock scotch eggs

Cook the eggs in a pan of boiling water – 2½–4 minutes depending on their size, then drain and submerge them in a bowl of ice-cold water to stop them cooking. Once they're cool, peel the eggs and set aside.

Bring the milk and garlic to the boil. Add the potatoes and thyme, reduce the heat and cook for 15–20 minutes, adding the fish to the pan for the last 10 minutes and poach until cooked through. Remove the pan from the heat and lift out the fish using a slotted spoon, leaving the potatoes to cool. Once cool, drain the potatoes, reserving a little of the milk. Remove and discard the thyme, then mash the potatoes. Flake in the fish and mix everything together well. If the mixture is too dry, add a little of the poaching milk. Season with salt and pepper.

Place a large spoonful (or 2 for hen's eggs) of the haddock mixture in the centre of a piece of clingfilm/plastic wrap and press out thinly with the back of a spoon. Place an egg in the centre of the potato and use the clingfilm/plastic wrap to pull the potato up and around the egg. Remove the clingfilm/plastic wrap and shape into a ball in your hands. Repeat the process with the remaining eggs and potato mixture. Chill for at least 30 minutes.

Put the breadcrumbs, flour and beaten eggs in separate shallow bowls. Heat the oil in a saucepan until it is hot enough to make a breadcrumb sizzle when dropped into it. Roll a haddock ball in the flour, then the beaten egg and finally the breadcrumbs to coat. Add the eggs to the pan in batches and cook for 2–3 minutes until golden brown, turning halfway through cooking.

These lighter dishes are perfect to enjoy for lunch or dinner. Combining grains such as quinoa and buckwheat with pulses, cheeses and fresh seasonal ingredients, makes light work of creating interesting and nutritious gluten-free meals.

light meals

creamy green soup

Chard, spinach, young kale, broccoli and even wild garlic and nettles can all be used to create this dazzling green soup! Avocado gives the recipe its creaminess and makes it filling, but boiled potatoes or a few spoons of dairy or rice cream can be substituted in the winter months.

5 handfuls of green leafy vegetables, such as chard, spinach, kale or nettles

¼ teaspoon salt

150 g/1 cup ripe avocado flesh

1 teaspoon freshly squeezed lemon juice

1 tablespoon olive oil

1 tablespoon red wine vinegar

1 teaspoon gluten-free soy sauce

3 garlic cloves, peeled and crushed

1 quantity Gluten-free Croutons (page 129)

Serves 3

Bring 1 litre/4 cups of water to a boil in a large saucepan. Carefully wash the greens and drain off the excess water. If using kale, remove the hard stem running up the centre of each leaf. Add the greens to the boiling water, cover and cook for 1–4 minutes, depending how soft the greens are – they should remain bright green in colour.

Add all the other ingredients except the croutons and then transfer the soup to a food processor and blend until smooth. Taste and adjust the seasoning if necessary.

Serve immediately with freshly made Gluten-free Croutons.

This delicious twist on a classic baked cheesecake makes the perfect midweek supper, served with a crisp green salad.

baked cheesecakes with salted honey walnuts

Crust

200 g/7 oz. gluten-free oatcakes, crushed

50 g/3½ tablespoons butter

3 tablespoons clear honey

salt and ground black pepper

Filling

150 g/⅔ cup cream cheese

150 g/⅔ cup ricotta cheese

75 ml/⅓ cup sour cream

1 teaspoon Dijon mustard

3 eggs, separated

100 g/3½ oz. Wensleydale, feta or any blue cheese, roughly chopped

a handful of chives, finely chopped

50g/¾ cup finely grated Parmesan

salt and ground white pepper

Salted honey walnuts

2 tablespoons clear honey

2 teaspoons brown sugar

2 teaspoons sea salt flakes, plus extra for sprinkling

100 g/¾ cup walnut pieces

4 chef's rings, greased

Serves 4

Preheat the oven to 180°C (350°F) Gas 4.

To make the crust, tip the oatcake crumbs into a large mixing bowl and season with salt and pepper. Melt the butter in a saucepan or pot set over gentle heat, until the butter foams and turns golden. Remove from the heat and stir in the honey until dissolved. Combine the butter and honey with the oatcake crumbs. Press the crumbs into the bottom of the chef's rings on top of a baking sheet. Bake the crust in the preheated oven for 8–10 minutes until golden and firm. Cool the oven to 160°C (325°F) Gas 3.

Meanwhile, put the cream cheese, ricotta, sour cream, mustard and egg yolks in a large mixing bowl and whisk until light and fluffy. Stir in the cheese and chives and season well. In a separate bowl, beat the egg whites to medium peaks. Take a spoonful of the egg white and stir it through the cheese mixture. Gently fold in the remaining egg whites with a metal spoon.

Spoon the mixture into the chef's rings to cover the oatcake crust, and sprinkle with the Parmesan. Bake in the still-warm oven for 30–40 minutes, until the cheesecakes are golden on top and set.

While they're cooking, make the salted honey walnuts. Put the honey, sugar and salt in a frying pan/skillet set over low heat. Stir until the sugar dissolves. Remove from the heat, add the walnut pieces and salt and stir until well coated. Transfer the nuts to a baking sheet, sprinkle with extra salt and leave to cool.

Use a knife to loosen the edges of the cheesecakes and turn them out. Serve warm, with the salted honey walnuts.

1 teaspoon cumin seeds

1 teaspoon coriander seeds

1 teaspoon mustard seeds

1 swede/rutabaga, trimmed, peeled and roughly chopped

2 large parsnips, trimmed, peeled and roughly chopped

1 tablespoon extra virgin olive oil, plus extra for roasting

salt and ground black pepper

2 tablespoons pure maple syrup

½ red onion

1–2 red chillies/chiles, deseeded

½ teaspoon ground turmeric

a handful of fresh parsley

3 eggs

2 small garlic cloves, peeled

1 teaspoon baking powder

2 teaspoons Dijon mustard

grated zest of 1 lemon

Parsley yogurt

300 ml/1¼ cups plain yogurt (or soy yogurt for a dairy-free option)

1 teaspoon agave syrup

1 teaspoon ground cumin

50 g/½ cup finely chopped fresh parsley

Serves 4–6

These fritters are great for using up vegetables lurking in your fridge. The combination of swede/rutabaga and parsnip is fantastic, but you could use any root vegetables you like.

root vegetable fritters

Preheat the oven to 200°C (400°F) Gas 6.

Put the cumin, coriander and mustard seeds in a dry frying pan/skillet and toast for 1–2 minutes until you can smell the aromas wafting up from the pan. Pound to a fine powder using a pestle and mortar.

Toss the chopped swede/rutabaga and parsnips in a large mixing bowl with a good glug of oil, a big pinch of salt, the maple syrup and half the toasted spices. Place in a roasting pan and roast in the preheated oven for 30 minutes, or until soft and slightly caramelized. Remove from the oven and allow to cool slightly.

Meanwhile, prepare the parsley yogurt by mixing all of the ingredients together. Set aside until you are ready to serve.

Spoon all the roasted ingredients, the onion, chillies/chiles, turmeric, parsley, eggs, garlic, baking powder, mustard and lemon zest into a food processor and blitz until quite smooth. Season with salt and pepper to taste.

In a large frying pan/skillet, heat 1 tablespoon oil over medium heat. Drop tablespoonfuls of the blitzed mixture into the pan and flatten into round shapes. Fry for a few minutes on each side or until golden. Handle gently when flipping over, as they don't firm up until fully cooked.

Serve the fritters with the sweet cumin and parsley yogurt and a green salad, if you like.

shaved broccoli and buckwheat salad

240 ml/1 cup vegetable stock

185 g/1 cup buckwheat groats

4 broccoli stalks

15 g/⅛ cup chopped hazelnuts

Dressing

300 g/1 cup plain yogurt

freshly squeezed juice of 2 lemons

½ teaspoon salt

½ teaspoon cumin powder

a bunch of fresh coriander/cilantro, chopped

Dukkah topping

2 teaspoons cumin seeds

2 teaspoons coriander seeds

1 teaspoon fennel seeds

100 g/¾ cup roasted hazelnuts, chopped*

100 g/¾ cup roasted sunflower seeds*

1 teaspoon sea salt

Serves 4–6

*see Note on page 75 for instructions on home roasting

Buckwheat, one of the great supergrains, works particularly well in this dish and makes a good alternative to bulgur or wheatberries for those on a gluten-free diet. Dukkah, made of crushed seeds, nuts and spices, is tasty and great for digestion too so it's win-win!

In a large saucepan or pot, put the vegetable stock, 240 ml/1 cup of water and the buckwheat groats over a medium–high heat. Bring to a boil, then turn down the heat and simmer for 15 minutes with the lid half on, stirring once halfway through. Be careful not to overcook the groats. Drain and rinse with cold water to cool.

Peel and shave the broccoli stalks into ribbons using a vegetable peeler or mandoline then add to a large saucepan or pot of boiling water. Cook for 3 minutes then shock the broccoli to suspend the cooking by submerging it in ice-cold water. Drain, cool and mix with the hazelnuts and reserved buckwheat.

For the dressing, whisk all the ingredients together and store in the refrigerator until you are ready to serve.

For the dukkah topping, use a pestle and mortar to grind the cumin, coriander and fennel seeds by hand. Blend the hazelnuts and sunflower seeds in a food processor to a roughly chopped consistency. Mix in a bowl with the crushed spices then set aside. This should yield about 200 g/1½ cups of dukkah.

To serve, spoon the broccoli and buckwheat mix onto individual plates, drizzle over the dressing and cover each serving with a tablespoon of dukkah topping.

160 g/1 cup polenta

100 g/1 cup grated courgette/zucchini

50 g/⅓ cup finely diced onion

70 g /½ cup finely grated smoked tofu

2–3 firm tomatoes

olive oil, for sprinkling and serving

½ teaspoon dried basil

salt and ground black pepper

fresh basil leaves, to garnish

a 35 x 25-cm/14 x 10-in. casserole dish or baking pan, well-oiled

Serves 2–3

Visually appealing and a song for your taste buds, this dish is crispy and full of summer flavours. The look and texture is similar to a traditional tarte flambée, without the bread base.

polenta tarte flambée

Preheat the oven to 200°C (400°F) Gas 6.

Bring 750 ml/3 cups of water to a boil, add ½ teaspoon salt and whisk in the polenta. Lower the heat, cover and let cook for 15 minutes. There's no need to stir. Lightly salt the grated courgette/zucchini, let sit for 5 minutes and then squeeze out as much of the water as you can. Add the onion, courgette/zucchini and grated smoked tofu to the cooked polenta and mix well. Add salt and pepper to taste.

Spoon the polenta mix into the oiled casserole dish or baking pan, evening the surface with a spatula or wet hands. Slice the tomatoes into 5-mm/⅕-in. thick slices and discard any excess juice and seeds. Arrange the tomato slices in a single layer over the top and sprinkle with olive oil, salt, dried basil and ground black pepper to taste.

Bake in the preheated oven for 20–25 minutes, or until golden brown and the tomatoes are sizzling. Let it cool a little, and then slice and serve with fresh basil and a generous splash of olive oil. Bon appétit!

300 g/1½ cups quinoa

2 teaspoons bouillon stock powder

salt and ground black pepper

12 asparagus spears, chopped in half

200 g/2 cups shelled broad/fava beans

200 g/2 cups peas

a handful of cherry tomatoes, halved

a large handful of fresh mint, roughly chopped

a handful of fresh parsley, roughly chopped

grated zest and freshly squeezed juice of 1 lemon

200 ml/¾ cup extra virgin olive oil

2 tablespoons agave syrup

1 tablespoon pomegranate molasses (or balsamic vinegar)

Serves 6

Quinoa is just as versatile as rice or gluten-free pasta for your daily cooking needs, if not more so. This simple dish is a celebration of new-season spring vegetables. At other times of the year, try different types of asparagus, ranging from white to crimson – they are great for adding a splash of colour.

quinoa with new-season beans, peas and asparagus

Put the quinoa and bouillon stock powder in a saucepan or pot and cover with just under double its volume of water. Bring to the boil, then reduce the heat to low and place the lid on top. Cook for about 12 minutes until all the water has been absorbed. Turn off the heat, remove the lid and let any remaining water evaporate. Transfer to a wide plate or baking dish to cool.

Meanwhile, bring a large pan of water to the boil and add 2 teaspoons of salt. Cook the asparagus, beans and peas separately in the boiling water, until just tender (about 3–4 minutes for each). You still want them to have a bit of bite.

Once the beans are cooked, they need to have their outer cases removed. Simply slide the pale case off each bean and discard.

In a large mixing bowl, gently but thoroughly mix the quinoa, asparagus, beans, peas, tomatoes and most of the herbs, reserving some for serving. Add the lemon zest and juice, oil, agave syrup and molasses, and season with salt and pepper. Mix again, taste and adjust the seasoning if necessary.

Serve in a large dish with the remaining herbs sprinkled on top and drizzled with oil.

Spanish bread salad

4 thick slices gluten-free bread (see pages 126–141)

3 tablespoons olive oil

2 garlic cloves, peeled

2 chorizo sausages, thinly sliced

1 red onion, thinly sliced

½ teaspoon Spanish smoked sweet paprika (pimentón dulce)

½ teaspoon dried thyme

a 410-g/14-oz. can chickpeas, rinsed and well drained

4 handfuls of baby spinach leaves

250 g/1½ cups cherry tomatoes, halved

2 tablespoons freshly squeezed lemon juice

salt and ground black pepper

a ridged stove-top grill pan or heavy cast-iron frying pan/skillet

Serves 4

Hidden in chorizo are spices that can be enticed out and used to flavour the oil it is cooked in. The warm, spiced pan juices are then tossed with the other ingredients so that the heat gently wilts the spinach. Try substituting chorizo with smoked bacon or pancetta and adding a little extra pimentón.

Preheat a grill pan over high heat.

Trim the crusts off the bread and discard. Brush both sides of the bread lightly with some of the oil. Place on the preheated pan and cook until golden and slightly charred on both sides. Rub the garlic cloves over the toasted bread and let cool. Tear into large chunks and set aside.

Heat the remaining oil in the pan. Add the chorizo slices and stir-fry for 2–3 minutes, until golden and aromatic. Add the onion, paprika and thyme and cook for 2–3 minutes, until softened. Transfer to a large serving bowl and pour in the seasoned oil from the pan. Add the toasted bread, chickpeas, spinach, tomatoes and lemon juice. Season to taste with salt and pepper and toss well to combine. Serve immediately.

Variation

For a vegetarian option, smoked tofu makes a good substitute for the chorizo, and tofu or vegetarian sausages also work well. Simply cook separately, slice and add to the finished dish.

black-eyed bean and red pepper salad with warm halloumi

300 g/1½ cups dried black-eyed beans/cow peas

3 fresh plum tomatoes, diced

1 red (bell) pepper, deseeded and diced

leaves from a bunch of fresh coriander/cilantro, chopped

65 ml/¼ cup olive oil

200 g/7 oz. halloumi cheese, cut into 2½-cm/1-in. pieces

2 tablespoons freshly squeezed lemon juice

1 tablespoon red wine vinegar

salt and ground black pepper

Serves 4

Halloumi cheese needs to be fried until golden in olive oil before being added to salads or enjoyed as part of a meze. It turns rubbery soon after cooking, so serve this salad as quickly as possible after making. If you can find bottled Spanish-style roasted peppers (pimientos) in oil, use them here, as they will add extra flavour.

Put the beans in a large mixing bowl, cover with cold water and let soak overnight.

Drain the beans and cook in a large saucepan or pot of simmering water for 1–1½ hours, until tender. Drain and transfer to a large bowl. Add the tomatoes, red (bell) pepper, coriander/cilantro and half of the oil.

Heat the remaining oil in a non-stick frying pan/skillet set over a high heat. Add the halloumi and cook for 3–4 minutes, turning often, until golden brown all over. Add to the bowl with the tomato mixture and stir in the lemon juice and vinegar. Season to taste and serve immediately.

Quinoa spaghetti is a very useful storecupboard staple and this recipe is super quick to make when you are short on time. The pepper flakes add a welcome spicy heat to the crab meat but this recipe also works well with tuna, if preferred.

quinoa spaghetti with chilli crab

125 g/5 oz dry quinoa spaghetti

2 garlic cloves, peeled and crushed

2 tablespoons olive oil

400 g/1 ⅓ cups canned chopped tomatoes

a pinch of dried chilli/hot red pepper flakes

80 g/½ cup fresh white crab meat or canned tuna, flaked

salt and ground black pepper, to taste

a handful of freshly chopped flat-leaf parsley, to garnish

Serves 2

Bring a large saucepan or pot of water to the boil over a high heat. Add the quinoa spaghetti and cook according to the packet instructions.

While the spaghetti is cooking, sauté the garlic in the olive oil in a medium–large frying pan/skillet set over a medium heat, until the garlic just begins to turn brown. Add the chopped tomatoes and dried chilli/hot red pepper flakes and cook for another few minutes. Reduce the heat and stir through the crab meat to just warm through.

Drain the spaghetti and add to the pan with the sauce. Gently mix the crab and tomato sauce with the spaghetti.

Serve the spaghetti on plates or in large pasta bowls, adding salt and pepper to taste, and garnish with flat-leaf parsley.

200 g/1 cup red quinoa

240 ml/1 cup vegetable stock

300 g/4½ cups sliced mushrooms

2 shallots, peeled and sliced

2 tablespoons vegetable oil

120 g/½ cup pulled pre-cooked chicken

a large bunch of freshly chopped flat-leaf parsley, to garnish

Harissa vinaigrette

3 teaspoons harissa paste

3 tablespoons flaxseed oil

3 tablespoons freshly squeezed lemon juice

1 tablespoon red wine vinegar

Serves 2

The textures and flavours in this salad are sure to impress. The combination of harissa, a North African hot red spice blend, and fresh parsley is delicious. You can prepare this salad in advance for when you know you will have leftover chicken, ready to assemble just before serving.

red quinoa chicken and mushroom salad

Put the quinoa in a large saucepan or pot with the vegetable stock and 220 ml/scant 1 cup of water over a medium–high heat. Bring to the boil then lower the heat, cover and simmer for 20 minutes. Remove from the heat, fluff with a fork, cover once more and let it sit in the pan for another 5 minutes. Remove the lid and set aside to cool.

While the quinoa cooks, sauté the mushrooms with the shallots in vegetable oil in a frying pan/skillet set over a medium heat for 8–10 minutes, or until the mushrooms are cooked. Remove from the heat and leave to cool.

For the vinaigrette, whisk all the ingredients together and set aside until you are ready to serve.

To serve, add the mushrooms and chicken to the quinoa. Toss to combine and pour over the dressing. Transfer to serving plates and garnish with the flat-leaf parsley.

buckwheat noodles with pak choi, cashews and tamari sauce

340 g/12 oz. gluten-free buckwheat noodles

1 onion, peeled and sliced

1 tablespoon finely chopped fresh ginger

1 tablespoon grapeseed oil

200 g/1 large head pak choi/bok choy, core removed

50 g/½ cup roasted cashew nuts (see Note)

Tamari sauce

1 tablespoon gluten-free soy sauce

2 teaspoons sesame oil

¼ teaspoon finely chopped fresh ginger

2 teaspoons flaxseed oil

2 teaspoons clear honey

1 tablespoon freshly squeezed lemon juice

1 tablespoon white sesame seeds

Serves 4

This is a great go-to Asian dish. Some brands of buckwheat noodles have wheat in them so do check the packaging very carefully before buying them.

Prepare the tamari sauce in advance. Whisk all of the ingredients together in a large bowl until combined.

Cook the noodles in a large saucepan or pot of salted water set over a medium heat for 10–12 minutes, or according to the packet instructions.

While the noodles are cooking, sauté the onion and ginger in the grapeseed oil until the onion is translucent. Add the chopped pak choi/bok choy, until wilted.

Drain the noodles, then mix together with the fried vegetables in the reserved bowl of tamari sauce. Toss with the cashew nuts and serve.

Note

If you can't find pre-roasted cashews you can roast them yourself by scattering them on an ungreased baking sheet and cooking in a preheated oven at 180°C (350°F) Gas 4 for 10 minutes, or until golden.

Comfort foods are perfect for darker evenings and filling up during the colder months. Here you'll find gluten-free recipes for the family favourites lasagne and pizza, as well as newer ideas such as a chicken tagine and slow-cooked pork belly.

home-cooked comforts

saffron and pepper frittata with roasted garlic aioli

200 g/7 oz. Desiree potatoes, peeled and chopped

2 tablespoons olive oil

½ white onion, finely sliced

1 garlic clove, peeled and crushed

a pinch of smoked paprika

a handful of frozen peas, defrosted

100 g/½ cup chopped roasted red (bell) peppers

4 eggs

a pinch of saffron strands, soaked in 1 tablespoon hot water

Aioli

1 garlic bulb

80 ml/⅓ cup olive oil

1 egg yolk

100 ml/scant 1 cup vegetable oil

a squeeze of fresh lemon juice

salt and ground black pepper

Serves 4

This filling potato frittata is bursting with flavour. If you don't have time to make the aioli yourself, simply stir the roasted garlic through a jar of store-bought gluten-free mayonnaise.

Preheat the oven to 200°C (400°F) Gas 6.

To make the aioli, cut about 1 cm/½ in. off the top of the garlic bulb so that the tops of the garlic cloves are exposed. Put the garlic, exposed cloves upwards, in the centre of a piece of foil. Drizzle with 2 tablespoons of the olive oil, then fold the foil around it to make a parcel. Bake in the preheated oven for 30–40 minutes until soft. Cool slightly before squeezing the cloves out of their skins into a bowl. Mash with a fork. Put the egg yolk in a small bowl with a pinch of salt. Slowly add the vegetable oil, drop by drop, whisking constantly, until it is all used up. Repeat with the remaining olive oil. If the mayonnaise becomes thick, add a little lemon juice to thin it out. Stir in the garlic and season to taste.

To make the frittata, boil the potatoes in a saucepan or pot of salted water until just cooked. Drain and cool before slicing thinly. Preheat the grill/broiler to medium. Heat the olive oil in a frying pan/skillet with a heatproof handle. Add the onion and cook over a low heat until softened. Add the crushed garlic and paprika and cook for 2 minutes. Add the peas, potatoes and peppers. Turn the heat up and stir until the ingredients are all evenly spread out. Beat the eggs with the saffron in a small mixing bowl. Season with salt and pepper, then pour the egg mixture into the pan and distibute evenly. Cook over high heat for 1 minute, then reduce the heat. Once the frittata is firm around the edges, transfer the pan to the grill/broiler and cook until the top is set and golden.

Serve the frittata in slices with the aioli on the side.

2 aubergines/eggplants, sliced lengthways

5 tablespoons olive oil

1 red onion, finely chopped

120 ml/½ cup white wine

1 carrot, finely chopped

1 red (bell) pepper, deseeded and finely chopped

½ courgette/zucchini, finely chopped

a handful of fresh dill, finely chopped

1 teaspoon dried oregano

1 teaspoon ground cinnamon

100 g/½ cup red lentils

400 g/2 cups canned chopped plum tomatoes

600 g/1 lb. 5 oz. potatoes, peeled and sliced

Topping

400 g/about 2 cups plain yogurt

2 eggs

grated zest of 1 lemon

a large pinch of grated nutmeg

60 g/½ cup crumbled feta cheese

salt and ground black pepper

Serves 4

Packed with nutritious ingredients, this satisfying gluten-free bake is popular with lovers of lasagne. It can be made ahead of time and is perfect for feeding the family or a crowd.

vegetable and lentil moussaka

Preheat the oven to 180°C (350°F) Gas 4.

Put the aubergine/eggplant slices in a baking dish, sprinkle with salt and 2 tablespoons olive oil, and bake in the preheated oven for 15–20 minutes, until soft and starting to brown.

Meanwhile, put the onion in a large saucepan or pot with 1 tablespoon of the olive oil and 1 tablespoon of water. Cover and cook over low heat for 5–10 minutes until the onion softens without taking on any colour. Remove the lid, add the wine and boil over high heat until the wine has reduced by half. Add the carrot, red (bell) pepper, courgette/zucchini, dill, oregano, and cinnamon, and fry until they turn golden brown. Add the lentils and tomatoes, along with 240 ml/1 cup of water and simmer over low heat for 20 minutes. Season with salt and pepper, to taste.

Fry the potatoes in the remaining 2 tablespoons of olive oil until they are golden on either side and the potato starts to soften. Remove from the pan and drain on paper towels.

To assemble the moussaka, lay half of the roasted aubergine/eggplant slices on the bottom of an ovenproof dish, cover with half of the lentil mixture and top with half of the potatoes. Repeat.

To make the topping, whisk the yogurt with the eggs, lemon, nutmeg and half of the feta. Pour on top of the moussaka and sprinkle the top with the remaining crumbled feta. Bake in the still-warm oven for 45 minutes until the top is golden brown.

This delicious recipe uses a basic and versatile gluten-free pasta recipe that is very useful to have in your repertoire.

lasagne

1 quantity Meat Ragu (page 91)

Cheese sauce

50 g/3½ tablespoons butter

1 tablespoon cornflour/cornstarch

500 ml/2 cups warm milk

200 g/2 cups grated Cheddar cheese

a pinch of grated nutmeg

salt and black pepper

Pasta

115 g/scant 1 cup yellow cornflour/fine cornmeal

60 g/½ cup quinoa flour

3 eggs, beaten

½ teaspoon salt

gluten-free plain/all-purpose flour, for dusting

a large ovenproof baking dish

a silicone mat (optional)

Serves 6–8

For the cheese sauce, melt the butter in a saucepan or pot set over a medium heat. Add the cornflour/cornmeal, cook for a minute, then gradually add the warm milk, a little at a time, stirring continuously until you have a smooth sauce. Add three-quarters of the cheese and stir until melted. Season with a little grated nutmeg, salt and pepper, then set aside to cool. Reserve the remaining cheese to sprinkle over the top of the lasagne.

Preheat the oven to 180°C (350°F) Gas 4. Set a pan of salted water to boil, ready to cook the pasta straight away. Spread half of the meat ragu over the base of the baking dish.

For the pasta, sift together the yellow cornflour/fine cornmeal and quinoa flour, then tip it into a mound on a silicone mat or clean work surface. Make a well in the middle and add the eggs and salt. Mix together with your fingertips until you have a soft dough.

Cut the dough into quarters, coat liberally in flour and then roll out each quarter, one by one, very thinly. Once rolled out, cut the dough into 15 cm x 8 cm/6 x 3½ in. rectangular sheets. As soon as they are rolled out, cook the pasta sheets, one at a time in the boiling water for about 2 minutes. Remove each sheet from the water with a slotted spoon and lay it on top of the meat. Repeat, rolling out and cooking enough pasta sheets to cover the bottom layer of meat. Cover the pasta with a layer of the cheese sauce and spread out thinly. Continue to roll out and cook more pasta sheets and layer them on top of the cheese sauce. Spoon the remaining meat ragu on top of the pasta and spread out evenly. Cover with the remaining cheese sauce and top with the reserved grated cheese. Sprinkle a little nutmeg and pepper over the top of the lasagne, then bake in the preheated oven for about 30–40 minutes until the cheese is golden brown on top.

polenta pizza

Polenta/cornmeal makes a great alternative to a traditional bread pizza base. This is a fantastic dish to share with friends.

2 teaspoons bouillon stock powder

200 g/1⅓ cups polenta/yellow cornmeal

grated zest and freshly squeezed juice of 1 lemon

5 garlic cloves, peeled and crushed

1 tablespoon fresh thyme leaves

salt and ground black pepper

1 head of chard, leaves separated

2 tablespoons extra virgin olive oil, plus extra to serve

200 g/7 oz. girolle/golden chanterelle mushrooms

1 tablespoon freshly chopped parsley

1 egg

a large baking sheet, oiled

Serves 2–4

Bring 1 litre/4 cups water to the boil and add the bouillon powder. Reduce the heat and slowly pour in the polenta/cornmeal, whisking all the time until blended. Reduce the heat to its lowest setting, add half the lemon zest and juice, 4 of the crushed garlic cloves, the thyme and a good pinch of salt and pepper and gently cook, stirring occasionally, for about 45 minutes or until the polenta pulls away from the side of the pan and is very thick.

Meanwhile, bring another pan of water to the boil. Add 1 teaspoon salt and cook the chard for 3–4 minutes until the thick part is just tender, but not limp. Remove, drain and season with extra salt and oil.

Heat 2 tablespoons oil in another pan over medium–high heat. Fry the mushrooms for 2 minutes, or until just golden and tender. Add the remaining crushed garlic clove and stir for 30 seconds to release the garlic flavour. Transfer to a bowl, toss with the parsley and season with salt, the remaining lemon zest and juice, and olive oil.

When the polenta is ready, spread it out to about 2 cm/¾ in. thick on the prepared baking sheet. Allow to cool for 30 minutes.

Preheat the grill/broiler.

Scatter the mushrooms and chard over the top of the polenta. Crack an egg carefully into the middle and grill/broil for 4–5 minutes or until the egg is cooked.

Remove from the grill/broiler, drizzle a little extra oil over the top and serve immediately.

2 teaspoons coriander seeds

6 chicken thighs, skin on and bone in

3 tablespoons extra virgin olive oil, plus extra for marinating

salt and ground black pepper

a good pinch of saffron threads

2 teaspoons ground cinnamon

1 teaspoon ground ginger

2 red onions, peeled and sliced

4 garlic cloves, peeled and crushed

3 tablespoons flaked/slivered almonds

2½-cm/1-in. piece of fresh ginger, peeled and finely chopped

1 cinnamon stick

12 Medjool dates, pitted/stoned and torn into halves

1 orange, rind peeled in strips

2 tablespoons pure maple syrup

4 tablespoons chopped fresh coriander/cilantro

1 preserved lemon

cooked quinoa or rice, to serve

Serves 4

The Moroccan spices and preserved lemon used here make for a really exotic dish. Tagines are very healthy, full of detoxing spices and dried and fresh fruit. You can of course swap the chicken for another meat, or make a vegetarian version with some kind of squash and green vegetable. Serve it on a bed of quinoa or the vibrant red Camargue rice.

chicken tagine

Put the coriander seeds in a dry frying pan/skillet and toast until fragrant. Pound to a fine powder using a pestle and mortar.

Rub the chicken thighs with a little oil, salt, pepper, the saffron threads, ground cinnamon, ground ginger and toasted coriander. Cover and marinate in the fridge for at least 1 hour, or overnight.

Heat 3 tablespoons oil in a tagine or casserole dish over medium heat. Add the onions, garlic, 2 tablespoons of the almonds, the fresh ginger, cinnamon stick and a good pinch of salt, and sweat until the onions are translucent, being careful not to burn the garlic. Transfer to a plate, and without washing the pan, add the chicken thighs. Turn up the heat to high and seal the skins, turning the chicken as it browns. When the chicken is golden all over, return the onion mixture to the pan. Pour in enough water to cover the chicken and bring to the boil. Reduce the heat, cover and simmer for 1 hour, stirring every so often.

Add the dates, orange peel, maple syrup and half the coriander/cilantro and simmer for 20 minutes, until the sauce is thick.

Rinse the preserved lemon well under running water. Scoop out and discard the flesh, and thinly slice the skin.

Plate up the quinoa or rice with the tagine on top. Sprinkle over the preserved lemon skin and remaining almonds and coriander/cilantro before serving.

Pastry

100 g/¾ cup rice flour

70 g/¾ cup cornflour/cornstarch

55 g/½ cup potato flour

1 teaspoon xanthan gum

a pinch of salt

50 g/3 tablespoons dairy-free butter, such as sunflower spread

60 g/¼ cup hard white vegetable shortening (it is crucial that you get the hardest one you can find)

1 egg, beaten with 1 teaspoon water

Filling

3 tablespoons extra virgin olive oil

3 leeks, trimmed and finely sliced

1 onion, peeled and sliced

3 garlic cloves, peeled and crushed

salt and ground black pepper

10 spears sprouting broccoli, trimmed

1 chorizo sausage, skinned and sliced

3 eggs

100 ml/6 tablespoons soy cream/creamer

a 20-cm/8-in. tart pan

baking beans

Serves 8–10

broccoli and chorizo tart

With the comforting baking smell that you get when cooking tarts, there are few who would turn down the offer of a slice.

To make the pastry, sift the flours, xanthan gum and salt into a large mixing bowl. Add the butter and shortening and cut into small chunks using a round-bladed knife. Trasfer the mixture to a food processor and blitz until it resembles breadcrumbs. Return the crumbs to the mixing bowl, add 1 tablespoon of the beaten egg and mix together with a fork. Bring the dough together with your hands to form a ball. If it is still crumbly, it needs a little more egg mixture. Wrap in clingfilm/plastic wrap and chill in the fridge.

Preheat the oven to 180°C (350°F) Gas 4.

Roll out the chilled pastry on a lightly floured surface to about 1 cm/⅜ in. thick, working quickly and handling it as little as possible. Line the tart pan with the pastry, making sure there are no cracks. Prick the base with a fork. Line the pastry case with baking parchment and fill with baking beans before blind-baking in the preheated oven for 20 minutes. Remove the parchment and beans, brush the base and sides of the shell with the remaining beaten egg and return to the oven for 5–10 minutes, until light brown. Increase the oven temperature to 200°C (400°F) Gas 6.

To make the filling, heat 3 tablespoons oil in a large saucepan or pot over medium heat. Add the leeks, onion, garlic and a good pinch of salt and pepper and cook until completely soft and translucent. Add the broccoli and cook for 10 minutes. Cook the chorizo in a separate dry pan until a little crispy and the fat has seeped out. Add to the leek and broccoli mixture and stir.

Add the filling mixture to the pastry case, reserving a little for the top of the tart. Beat the eggs together with the cream and pour into the pastry case. Scatter the reserved ingredients over the top and bake the tart in the preheated oven for 30–35 minutes, until the top is firm.

beef and courgette gratin

It's not possible to have too many recipes for beef mince, and this is a great one (see the Lasagne on page 83 for an alternative recipe that also uses this meat ragu). The goat's cheese lifts this out of the ordinary but, as the flavour is not to everyone's taste, strong Cheddar is a nice option if you prefer.

6 courgettes/zucchini, sliced

225 g/1 cup half-fat crème fraîche

60 g/¼ cup soft goat's cheese

110 g/1 cup grated Gruyère or Cheddar cheese

1–2 tablespoons whole milk

olive oil, for frying

salt and ground black pepper

Meat ragu

1 onion, peeled and finely sliced

1 teaspoon each of dried thyme and dried oregano

¼ teaspoon dried chilli/hot red pepper flakes

2 garlic cloves, peeled and crushed

125 ml/½ cup white or red wine

500 g/2¼ cups ground beef mince

400 g/2 cups canned chopped tomatoes

a pinch of sugar

a 25 x 20-cm/10 x 8-in. baking dish

Serves 4–6

For the meat ragu, cook the onion in 1 tablespoon of the oil over a medium heat for 3–5 minutes, until soft. Stir in the thyme, oregano, chilli/hot red pepper flakes and garlic and cook, stirring, for about 1 minute. Add the wine, cook for a further minute, then add the beef. Cook for 5–8 minutes, stirring occasionally, until the beef is browned. Stir in the tomatoes and sugar and season well. Reduce the heat, cover, and simmer gently for at least 15 minutes.

Preheat the oven to 200°C (400°F) Gas 6.

Meanwhile, prepare the courgettes. Line a tray with paper towels. Working in batches, heat some of the oil in a large non-stick frying pan. When hot, add the courgette rounds and fry, in a single layer. When just golden, turn and brown the other side. Transfer to the lined tray. Continue until all the courgettes are browned.

Stir 2 tablespoons of the crème fraîche into the beef mixture. Put the remaining crème fraîche in a bowl, crumble in the goat's cheese and season with salt and pepper. Mix well. Set aside.

To assemble, arrange one-third of the courgettes in an even layer on the bottom of the baking dish. Sprinkle with salt and one-third of the grated cheese. Top with half of the beef mixture, spread evenly. Repeat the courgette and beef layer. Finish with a final courgette layer. Season with salt, then spread with an even layer of the crème fraîche topping. Sprinkle over the remaining cheese. Bake in the preheated oven for about 30 minutes, until the top is golden brown.

1 onion, peeled and sliced

2 garlic cloves

1 celery stalk, chopped

leaves from a small bunch of fresh parsley

2 tablespoons olive oil

750 g/3¾ cup beef mince

350 g/1¾ cup pork mince

2 eggs, beaten

2 tablespoons milk

100 g/1¼ cups fresh gluten-free breadcrumbs (see Note)

1 teaspoon dried thyme

2 teaspoons salt

½ teaspoon ground white pepper

1 teaspoon paprika

60 ml/¼ cup chilli/chile sauce or tomato ketchup

2–3 bay leaves, plus extra to garnish

5–6 streaky bacon rashers/strips

a shallow roasting pan

Serves 6–8

Perfect for feeding the family, this American classic simply must be served with a pile of fluffy mashed potatoes and plenty of hot gravy for pouring. Any leftovers make the perfect cold sandwich filling the next day, with the addition of a tangy vegetable pickle or chutney.

meatloaf

Preheat the oven to 180°C (350°F) Gas 4.

Combine the onion, garlic, celery and parsley in a food processor and pulse until minced.

Transfer the mixture to a frying pan/skillet, add the oil and cook over low heat for 5–7 minutes, until soft. Transfer to a large mixing bowl and add the beef, pork, eggs, milk, breadcrumbs, thyme, salt, pepper, paprika and chilli/chile sauce. Mix well with your hands until well blended.

Form the mixture into an oval loaf shape, as if you were making bread. Put the bay leaves in the middle of the roasting pan and place the meatloaf on top. Arrange the bacon slices on top, at equal intervals, and tuck carefully under the bottom of the loaf.

Bake in the preheated oven for about 1½ hours, until browned and cooked through. Check the meatloaf regularly and baste with the pan juices to keep it moist. Serve with mashed or roast potatoes and gravy.

Note

The best way to obtain fresh breadcrumbs is to use the end pieces from a sliced loaf, but nothing with seeds. Simply tear into smaller pieces and blitz in a food processor to make crumbs. The food processor is required for the onions in this recipe as well, but do the breadcrumbs first because they are a dry ingredient.

This comforting yet elegant supper dish can be prepared the night or morning before serving. Simply assemble the gratin, up to the point of pouring on the cream, cover and refrigerate.

salmon, broccoli and potato gratin with pesto

975 g/2 lbs. waxy potatoes, peeled

a large head of broccoli (about 480 g/1 lb.), separated into florets

400 g/14 oz. boneless, skinless salmon fillet

1 tablespoon olive oil

20 g/3 tablespoons fresh gluten-free breadcrumbs (see Note on page 92)

4 tablespoons freshly grated Parmesan

250 ml/1 cup single/light cream

2 tablespoons green pesto

4 tablespoons milk

2–3 tablespoons butter, cut into small pieces

salt and ground black pepper

a 25-cm/10-in. baking dish, well buttered

Serves 4–6

Preheat the oven to 200°C (400°F) Gas 6.

Put the potatoes in a large saucepan or pot and cover with cold water. Parboil until almost tender when pierced with a knife. Drain. When cool enough to handle, slice into 3-mm/⅛-in. thick rounds.

Bring another saucepan or pot of water to the boil. Add the broccoli and a pinch of salt and cook for 3–4 minutes, until just tender. Drain and let cool. Cut into bite-sized pieces and set aside.

Rub the salmon fillets with the oil and place on a sheet of foil, turned up at the sides to catch any juices. Transfer to a baking sheet and sprinkle with a little salt. Bake in the preheated oven for about 10–15 minutes, until cooked through. Let cool, then flake into a bowl and set aside.

In a small bowl, mix together the breadcrumbs and 2 tablespoons of the Parmesan. Season well and set aside. In another bowl, stir together the cream and pesto. Season well and set aside.

To assemble, arrange the potato slices on the bottom of the prepared baking dish in an even layer. Sprinkle with salt, plus the remaining Parmesan and drizzle with the milk. Arrange the broccoli in an even layer on top of the potatoes and season lightly. Top with the cooked salmon in an even layer.

Pour over the pesto and cream mixture. Sprinkle the breadcrumb mixture over the top and dot with butter. Bake in the preheated oven for 25–30 minutes, until just browned and crisp on top.

chicken and sweet potato pot pie

1½ kg/3½ lbs. sweet potatoes, peeled and cut into chunks

3–4 tablespoons olive oil, plus extra for frying

2–4 tablespoons butter

1 onion, diced

100 g/4 oz. bacon, chopped

150 g/2 cups mushrooms, chopped

2 celery sticks, chopped

2 garlic cloves, peeled and crushed

2 teaspoons dried thyme

75–100 g/2½–3½ oz. cooked sausages, chopped

100 g/¾ cup vacuum-packed peeled chestnuts, chopped

a large handful of freshly chopped parsley

½ a cooked chicken (about 700 g/ 1½ lbs.), shredded

125 g/4 oz. stale or toasted gluten-free bread, broken into small pieces

5 tablespoons milk

180 ml/¾ cup chicken stock

salt and ground black pepper

a 25–30 cm/10–12 in. round baking dish, well buttered

Serves 4–6

Sweet potato mash makes a nice change from potato mash. Here it pairs very nicely with chicken in this ingenious recipe which is designed as a way to use up leftover roast chicken, but you could also buy a supermarket rotisserie chicken.

Preheat the oven to 220°C (425°F) Gas 7.

Toss the sweet potatoes with the oil and arrange in a single layer on a baking sheet. Roast in the preheated oven for about 45 minutes, until tender and browned. Reduce the oven temperature to 200°C (400°F) Gas 6.

Let the sweet potatoes cool, then peel, mash with butter to taste and season with salt. Set aside.

Heat a little more oil in a frying pan/skillet. Add the onion and cook for 2–3 minutes, until soft. Season with salt, then add the bacon, mushrooms and celery, and cook for 3–5 minutes, stirring often. Add the garlic, thyme, sausages and chestnuts, and cook for about 1 minute. Stir in the parsley and chicken and set aside.

In a bowl, combine the bread pieces and milk and toss to coat. The bread should be moist; you may need to add more milk. Add the bread to the chicken mixture, along with the stock. Stir well. Taste and adjust the seasoning.

Spread the chicken mixture in an even layer in the prepared baking dish. It will dry out slightly with baking, so if it seems dry at the outset, add a bit more of any liquid: stock, milk or water. Top with the mashed sweet potato and spread evenly. Bake in the preheated oven for about 45 minutes – the sweet potato won't brown but should start to blacken slightly where peaked.

slow-cooked pork belly with beans and miso

100 g/⅔ cup cooked small white beans, such as cannellini or navy beans, drained and rinsed

1 kg/2¼ lbs. pork belly, in 1 piece

125 ml/½ cup sake (Japanese rice wine)

1 tablespoon peanut oil

2 teaspoons sesame oil

3 garlic cloves, peeled and roughly chopped

4 spring onions/scallions, white parts only, chopped

5 thin slices fresh ginger

250 ml/1 cup chicken or vegetable stock

2 tablespoons gluten-free light soy sauce

2 tablespoons white miso/shinshu (soya bean paste)

1 teaspoon sugar

½ teaspoon salt

a large casserole dish

Serves 4

In China, soya beans are known as the 'meat of the earth' because of their high nutritional value. They are, however, quite bland so need the robust Asian flavours alongside them.

Cut the pork belly into 8 pieces. Put the pieces in a large dish and pour over the sake. Cover with clingfilm/plastic wrap and set aside for 1 hour, turning often. Remove the pork from the sake, reserving the sake.

Put the peanut oil in a casserole dish and set over a high heat. Cook the pork in batches, so as not to overcrowd the pan, for 4–5 minutes, turning often, until golden all over. Put the browned pork in a bowl and set aside.

Preheat the oven to 160°C (325°F) Gas 3.

Add the sesame oil to the casserole dish with the garlic, spring onions/scallions and ginger and stir-fry for 1–2 minutes, until aromatic and softened.

Add the reserved sake, letting it boil, and cook until the liquid has reduced by half, stirring to remove any stuck-on bits of pork from the bottom of the dish. Add the stock, soy sauce, miso/shinshu, sugar and salt and return the pork to the pan, stirring until the miso/shinshu dissolves.

Bring to the boil, cover with a tight-fitting lid, transfer to the preheated oven and cook for 2 hours, turning the pork after 1 hour. Stir in the beans, cover and cook for 30 minutes more. Serve hot.

There is no need to miss out on sweet treats when you are gluten-free. Cater for a sweet tooth with recipes including white chocolate and walnut brownies, caramel shortbread, olive oil and orange cake, and lemon and ginger cheesecake. Yum!

treats

white chocolate and walnut brownies

250 g/2 sticks plus 2 tablespoons butter

300 g/10½ oz. dark/bittersweet chocolate (70% cocoa solids)

300 g/1½ cups plus 1 tablespoon caster/granulated sugar

200 g/1½ cups soft dark brown sugar

5 large eggs

1 teaspoon pure vanilla extract

100 g/¾ cup gluten-free self-raising/rising flour (or a generous 100 g/ ¾ cup gluten-free plain/all-purpose flour, plus 1 teaspoon baking powder and ½ teaspoon xanthan gum)

200 g/2 cups shelled walnuts, finely ground

150 g/1 cup gluten-free white chocolate buttons

a 33 x 23-cm/13 x 9-in. baking pan, greased and lined with baking parchment

Makes 20 brownies

These moist, crumbly brownies are quite literally melt in the mouth. Walnuts are ground finely and used in place of some of the flour, which gives the brownies a wonderfully nutty flavour.

Preheat the oven to 190°C (375°F) Gas 5.

Melt the butter and dark chocolate in a heatproof bowl set over a pan of simmering water or in a microwave-proof bowl in the microwave on high power for 1 minute, and stir to ensure there are no lumps. Set aside to cool.

Whisk the caster/granulated sugar and dark brown sugar with the eggs and vanilla extract until the mixture is very light and has doubled in size. Whilst still whisking, slowly pour in the melted chocolate and butter mixture. Fold in the flour and ground walnuts, then pour the mixture into the prepared tin/pan. Sprinkle over the chocolate buttons (which should sink into the mixture) ensuring that they are evenly distributed.

Bake in the preheated oven for about 30–40 minutes, until the brownies have formed a crust and a knife inserted into the middle of the tin/pan comes out clean with no cake batter on it. Allow to cool before cutting into squares.

These brownies will keep for up to 5 days if stored in an airtight container.

160 g/1⅓ cups gluten-free self-raising/rising flour (or 160 g/1⅓ cups gluten-free plain/all-purpose baking flour, plus 1½ teaspoons baking powder and ¾ teaspoon xanthan gum)

1 teaspoon bicarbonate of/baking soda

180 g/2 cups ground almonds

180 g/1 cup caster/granulated sugar

2 teaspoons ground ginger

grated zest of 2 limes

125 g/1 stick plus 1 tablespoon butter

6 balls stem ginger in syrup, finely chopped, plus 3 tablespoons ginger syrup

2 baking sheets, greased and lined with baking parchment

Makes about 18 cookies

Ginger cookies are perfect on a cold day. Warming pieces of ginger and tangy lime always soothe away life's troubles. If you prefer, you can replace the lime zest with orange zest and a pinch of cinnamon for a more festive feel. These cookies store well in an airtight container or can be used as the base of Lemon and Ginger Cheesecake on page 124.

ginger cookies

Preheat the oven to 180°C (350°F) Gas 4.

Put the flour, bicarbonate of soda/baking soda, ground almonds, caster sugar, ground ginger and lime zest in a mixing bowl and mix together. Put the butter and ginger syrup in a small saucepan and heat gently until the butter has melted. Let cool slightly and then stir into the dry ingredients, along with the chopped ginger. Put about 18 tablespoonfuls of the mixture on the prepared baking sheets, leaving a gap between each, as the cookies will spread during cooking. (You may need to bake in batches, depending on the size of your baking sheets.)

Bake in the preheated oven for about 12–15 minutes, until the cookies are golden brown. Leave to cool on the baking sheets for a few minutes then transfer to a wire rack with a spatula to cool.

These cookies will keep for up to 5 days if stored in an airtight container.

Shortbread base

115 g/1 stick butter, softened

60 g/⅓ cup caster/granulated sugar

85 g/¾ cup gluten-free self-raising/rising flour (or 85 g/¾ cup gluten-free plain/all-purpose baking flour, plus 1 teaspoon baking powder and ⅛ teaspoon xanthan gum)

85 g/1 cup ground almonds

Caramel layer

60 g/⅓ cup caster/granulated sugar

60 g/½ stick butter

300 g/1 cup condensed milk

1 teaspoon pure vanilla extract

Chocolate topping

150 g/5½ oz milk/semisweet chocolate

a 20-cm/8-in. square baking tin/pan, greased and lined with baking parchment

Makes 16 shortbreads

Caramel or millionaire's shortbread is always popular. What's not to like about a buttery cookie base with a layer of gooey caramel topped with chocolate. You can replace the milk/semisweet chocolate topping with dark/bittersweet or gluten-free white chocolate if you prefer and decorate with gluten-free sprinkles for a pretty party effect.

caramel shortbread

Preheat the oven to 180°C (350°F) Gas 4.

To make the shortbread base, put the butter and sugar in a mixing bowl and cream together. Sift in the flour then add the almonds and bring the mixture together with your hands to form a soft dough. Press into the prepared tin/pan and prick all over with a fork. Bake in the preheated oven for 15–20 minutes, until the shortbread is golden brown. Let cool in the tin/pan.

For the caramel layer, put the sugar, butter, condensed milk and vanilla extract in a small saucepan and warm over gentle heat until the butter has melted and the sugar dissolved. Bring to the boil, beating all the time so that the mixture doesn't stick, then reduce the heat and simmer for about 5 minutes, until golden brown and thick. Pour over the shortbread base and let cool.

To make the chocolate topping, put the chocolate in a heatproof bowl set over a saucepan of barely simmering water and stir gently until melted. Pour the chocolate over the caramel and leave to set. Use a hot knife to cut into 16 squares to serve.

These shortbreads will keep for up to 5 days if stored in an airtight container.

fruit and nut flapjacks

100 g/6½ tablespoons coconut oil

20 g/4 teaspoons sunflower spread

130 ml/½ cup sunflower oil

2 ripe bananas, peeled and mashed

2 teaspoons pure vanilla extract

140 g/¾ cup sugar or coconut palm sugar

60 ml/¼ cup agave syrup or runny honey

1 tablespoon date syrup, golden syrup or corn syrup

a good pinch of salt

500 g/4 cups gluten-free rolled oats

150 g/1 cup (dark) raisins

100 g/¾ cup pumpkin seeds

60 g/½ cup pecans

100 g/⅔ cup dried apricots, chopped

a 20–25 cm/8–10 in. baking pan

Serves 10–12

These deliciously chewy flapjacks are intoxicatingly buttery-tasting and sticky with syrup while still being nutritious.

Preheat the oven to 180°C (350°F) Gas 4.

Gently heat the coconut oil, sunflower spread, sunflower oil, bananas, vanilla extract, xylitol or coconut sugar, agave syrup, date syrup and salt in a saucepan just until the sunflower spread has melted. Whisk the mixture together until smooth.

In a large mixing bowl, combine the oats, raisins, pumpkin seeds, pecans and apricots. Add the molten mixture from the pan and mix very well. Spoon the mixture into the baking pan and flatten down tightly to help it hold together. Bake in the preheated oven for about 25 minutes or until the flapjacks are a lovely golden, light brown colour. If it looks like they are colouring too quickly, turn the heat down to 160°C (325°F) Gas 3. The main thing is not to burn the top, as the raisins and apricots burn easily and become very bitter.

With flapjacks, you really can make them your own. If you are less keen on the dried fruit, take it out or add other nuts or seeds. The choice is yours.

2 eggs

200 ml/1 cup coconut milk

70 g/½ cup vegetable oil

300 g/2 cups dark/bittersweet chocolate, melted

1 teaspoon pure vanilla extract

40 g/⅓ cup brown rice flour

40 g/⅓ cup teff flour (available online)

45 g/⅓ cup potato starch

2 tablespoons flaxseeds

1 teaspoon xanthan gum

¾ teaspoon baking powder

¾ teaspoon bicarbonate of/ baking soda

50 g/½ cup cocoa powder

1 teaspoon espresso powder

100 g/½ cup sugar or coconut palm sugar

Almond butter icing

80 ml/⅓ cup coconut oil

60 ml/¼ cup smooth unsalted almond butter

375 g/3 cups icing/confectioners' sugar

3–6 teaspoons almond milk

1 teaspoon pure vanilla extract

a 12-hole muffin pan lined with 9 paper cases

Makes 9

Here is a rich chocolate cupcake using a high percentage of wholegrain flours as its base that proves you can have your gluten-free cake and eat it too!

chocolate cupcakes with almond butter icing

Preheat the oven to 180°C (350°F) Gas 4.

Put all of the wet ingredients into a mixing bowl and whisk until smooth. Sift the dry ingredients into a separate mixing bowl then add the wet to the dry mixture a little at a time. Whisk until completely smooth and mixed together. Spoon the mix into the prepared muffin pan. Bake for 20 minutes until a toothpick comes out clean. Leave to cool on a wire rack.

For the icing, beat the coconut oil and almond butter together very quickly until well combined. Add 125 g/1 cup of the icing/confectioners' sugar with a teaspoon of almond milk and stir in slowly. Add the vanilla and continue to add a little of the sugar and milk to the mixture at a time, keeping the consistency thick and fluffy.

buttermilk scones

The classic scone is so simple to make and always popular. Filled with cream and fruit preserve, these scones represent everything that is lovely about the British summertime.

350 g/2½ cups plus 1 tablespoons gluten-free self-raising/rising flour plus 2 teaspoons baking powder (or 350 g/2½ cups plus 1 tablespoon gluten-free plain/all-purpose flour, plus 4 teaspoons baking powder and 1 teaspoon xanthan gum), plus extra for dusting

100 g/1¼ cups ground almonds

115 g/1 stick butter

60 g/⅓ cup caster/granulated sugar, plus extra for sprinkling

2 teaspoons pure almond extract

200–250 ml/¾–1 cup buttermilk

milk, for glazing

To serve

300 g/1 cup clotted cream

3 generous tablespoons strawberry preserve

a baking sheet, greased and lined with baking parchment

a 7½-cm/3-in. fluted cookie cutter

Makes 12

Preheat the oven to 190°C (375°F) Gas 5.

Put the flour, baking powder and ground almonds in a mixing bowl and rub in the butter with your fingertips. Add the sugar and almond extract and mix in the buttermilk, until you have a soft dough (you may not need all of it, so add it gradually).

Roll out the dough on a lightly floured surface to about 2–3 cm/¾–1¼ in. thick. Stamp out 12 rounds using the cutter. Arrange them on the prepared baking sheet so that they are a distance apart. Brush the tops of each round with milk and sprinkle with a little caster/granulated sugar. Bake in the preheated oven for 15–20 minutes, until golden brown and the scones sound hollow when you tap them. Transfer to a wire rack to cool.

To serve, cut the scones in half, spoon some cream on the base of each one, top with strawberry preserve and cover with the tops of the scones. They are best eaten on the day they are made but can be frozen and reheated before serving.

Variation
Try adding 85 g/½ cup dried cherries, sultanas/golden raisins or chocolate chips to the scone dough (replacing the almond extract with vanilla extract).

buckwheat and cherry cake

6 large eggs, separated

200 g/1 cup caster/superfine sugar

100 g/¾ cup buckwheat flour

2 teaspoons baking powder

kirsch, for drizzling (optional)

600 ml/2½ cups double/heavy cream, whipped to soft peaks

300 g/1 cup bottled or canned sour/tart morello cherries (drained weight)

3 tablespoons grated dark/bittersweet chocolate

a 23-cm/9-in. springform cake pan, greased and lined with baking parchment

Serves 8–10

Discover the delights of buckwheat cake, delicate layers of almost marshmallow-like sponge filled with whipped cream and sour cherries. This is a northern German twist on the classic and ever-popular Black Forest Gâteau.

Preheat the oven to 180°C (350°F) Gas 4.

Whisk together the egg yolks and sugar until thick, pale and creamy. In a separate grease-free bowl, whisk the egg whites to stiff peaks. Gently fold the egg whites into the egg yolk mixture. Mix together the flour and baking powder. Sift over the egg mixture and gently fold in.

Pour the batter into the prepared baking pan. Bake in the preheated oven for 30–40 minutes, until the cake is firm to the touch. It will feel foam-like rather than cake-like – almost like a giant marshmallow.

Carefully turn the cake out from the tin/pan onto a wire rack and let cool completely. Using a large, sharp knife, slice the cake into three layers. Drizzle each layer with kirsch, if using.

Assemble the cake, filling each layer with whipped cream and cherries. Top the final layer with grated chocolate and serve immediately or cover and refrigerate until needed.

This cake is best eaten on the day it is made as it contains fresh cream. Store in the fridge until ready to serve.

225 g/2 sticks butter, softened

170 g/1 cup caster/granulated sugar

85 g/¾ cup dark brown sugar

100 g/⅓ cup gluten-free marzipan

4 eggs

115 g/1 scant cup gluten-free self-raising/rising flour (or 115 g/ 1 scant cup gluten-free plain/all-purpose flour, plus 1 teaspoon baking powder and ½ teaspoon xanthan gum)

200 g/2½ cups ground almonds

100 g/½ cup (about 6 pieces) stem ginger in syrup, finely chopped

6 tablespoons buttermilk

icing/confectioners' sugar, for dusting

Poached pears

5 tall ripe pears, peeled

80 ml/⅓ cup ginger syrup

100 ml/⅓ cup ginger wine

100 g/½ cup caster/granulated sugar

½ vanilla pod/bean, scored lengthways and seeds scraped

2 balls stem ginger

a 23-cm/9-in springform cake pan, greased and lined with baking parchment

Serves 10

When ripe pears are in season they make delicious desserts. Here they are poached in ginger and vanilla and nestled in a moist almond sponge. Perfection.

pear and almond sponge

Put the pears in a saucepan or pot with the ginger syrup, ginger wine, sugar, vanilla pod/bean and seeds, stem ginger and enough water so that the pears just float. Simmer over a gentle heat for 20–30 minutes, until the pears are soft. Leave them to cool in the poaching liquid until completely cold. Scoop out the cores from the base of each pear using a melon baller. Discard the cores, return the pears to the poaching liquid and set aside.

Preheat the oven to 180°C (350°F) Gas 4.

Put the butter and both sugars in a large mixing bowl and whisk together. Cut the marzipan into small pieces and mix into the butter mixture. Add the eggs one at a time, whisking after each addition, until the batter is light and airy. Sift in the flour and add the almonds, stem ginger and buttermilk. Whisk until everything is incorporated. Spoon the batter into the prepared baking pan.

Drain the pears and arrange them upright in a ring in the pan, pushing each pear all the way down into the cake batter.

Bake in the preheated oven for 35–45 minutes, checking halfway through cooking to ensure that the pears are still upright, adjusting them if they have slipped. If the cake starts to brown too much, cover loosely with kitchen foil. Let cool in the pan. Dust with icing/ confectioners' sugar and cut the cake so that each slice contains half a pear.

olive oil and orange cake

1 large orange

1 large lemon

100 ml/⅓ cup fruity extra virgin olive oil

175 g/¾ cup plus 2 tablespoons caster/granulated sugar

4 eggs

175 g/1¾ cups ground almonds

2 teaspoons baking powder

icing/confectioners' sugar, to dust

a 20-cm/8-in. loose-bottomed cake pan, greased and base-lined with baking parchment

Serves 8–10

There are fantastic results to be had from using oils rather than hard fats in cakes. This cake is extremely moist yet has a light-as-air texture and a gorgeous orangey flavour. Perfect as a teatime treat, it also makes a lovely after-dinner dessert when served with red berries.

Wash the orange and lemon and put them both in a large saucepan or pot. Cover with water, bring to the boil, then simmer for 30 minutes or so, until soft. Remove the fruit from the water and leave to cool. Cut the orange and lemon in half, discard any pips and put the skin and pulp in a food processor. Blitz to a purée/paste and set aside.

Preheat the oven to 180°C (350°F) Gas 4.

Beat the olive oil, sugar and eggs together until light and fluffy. Stir in the ground almonds and baking powder. Add the puréed fruit and stir until thoroughly mixed. Spoon the batter into the prepared cake pan.

Bake in the preheated oven for 50–60 minutes, or until the cake is golden and risen and springs back when touched with a fingertip. Leave to cool in the tin until completely cold. Turn out and dust with icing/confectioners' sugar.

Serve in slices with fresh berries, if desired.

vanilla ice cream or frozen yogurt,
to serve (optional)

Filling

2 cooking apples, peeled, cored
and roughly chopped

2 pears, peeled, cored and roughly
chopped

80 g/scant ½ cup sugar or
coconut palm sugar

freshly squeezed juice of ½ lemon

60 g/½ cup pecans, lightly
roasted

Topping

30 g/2 tablespoons sunflower
spread

30 g/2 tablespoons coconut oil

70 g/½ cup plus 1 tablespoon rice
flour

70 g/½ cup gluten-free rolled oats

60 g/⅓ cup sugar or coconut
palm sugar

2 tablespoons pure maple syrup

1 teaspoon ground cinnamon

a medium casserole dish

Serves 6–8

There's nothing better than the smell of apple crumble baking
in the oven – is all about: indulgence, warmth, familiarity and
home comforts. Serve it in generous portions with a scoop of
ice cream or frozen yogurt.

pear and apple pecan crumble

To make the filling, toss the chopped apples and pears in a large
saucepan with the coconut sugar, lemon juice and 1 tablespoon
water. Stew over low–medium heat until half cooked. Taste and
add more coconut sugar if necessary. Transfer to the casserole
dish with all the juices and mix in the pecans, reserving some for
the top. Allow to cool while you prepare the topping.

Preheat the oven to 180°C (350°F) Gas 4.

To make the topping, rub the sunflower spread and coconut
oil into the flour in a large mixing bowl, until it resembles fine
breadcrumbs. Add the oats, sugar, maple syrup and cinnamon
and mix thoroughly.

Sprinkle the topping over the filling in the dish and bake in the
preheated oven for 35–45 minutes, or until the fruit is tender
and the juices are bubbling. Sprinkle the remaining pecans over
the top and serve with a scoop of icecream or frozen yogurt,
if desired.

100 g/3½ oz. best-quality dark/bittersweet chocolate (70% cocoa solids)

Base

10 pitted dates

150 g/1 cup pecans, lightly roasted

125 g/4 oz. gluten-free oat cakes

1 teaspoon pure vanilla extract

2 tablespoons agave syrup

2 tablespoons coconut oil

3 teaspoons unsweetened cocoa powder

Filling

3 avocados, not too firm

6 tablespoons agave syrup

1 tablespoon carob powder

5 tablespoons unsweetened cocoa powder

2 teaspoons pure vanilla extract

3 tablespoons date syrup

½ teaspoon salt

4 tablespoons coconut oil

a 20-cm/8-in. springform cake pan, greased and base-lined with baking parchment

Serves 10–12

Convincing people that food, especially desserts, made without wheat, dairy and (in this case) sugar can actually taste good, let alone delicious, is an almost impossible task. Not so with this chocolate tart. It will convert even the greatest cynics!

chocolate tart

To make the base, blitz the dates in a food processor, then add the rest of the ingredients and a pinch of salt, and blitz until everything comes together in a sticky ball. Press into the baking pan so that you have an even and smooth base for the tart. Refrigerate for 30 minutes or freeze for 15 minutes to set.

To make the filling, cut the avocados in half, remove the stones and scoop the flesh into a food processor. Add the remaining ingredients, excluding the coconut oil, and blitz until smooth.

Melt the coconut oil in a saucepan or pot over a very low heat – this will only take a few moments. With the motor running, pour the coconut oil into the filling mixture. Once combined, pour the mixture onto the set tart base and smooth out the top. Refrigerate for at least 2 hours or if you want it to set quickly, freeze it.

When you are ready to serve, warm the chocolate to just above room temperature to make it easier to grate. I find leaving it beside the oven when you are cooking for about 10 minutes does the trick. You want the chocolate to be just beginning to soften – not in any way gooey or melting, just not rock solid, so it grates easily in long strips.

Pop the tart out of the baking pan and transfer to a plate. Liberally grate the chocolate over, so it piles up high. The tart should be served fridge-cold so that it stays reasonably firm. It keeps wonderfully well and can easily be made a day in advance.

lemon and ginger cheesecake

Lemon and ginger are the perfect combination. This indulgent cheesecake is studded with stem ginger pieces that contrast beautifully with the tangy lemon curd.

(see page 104)

Crumb case

300 g/10½ oz. Ginger Cookies (see page 104) or store-bought gluten-free ginger cookies

150 g/1¼ sticks butter, melted

Topping

60 g/4 tablespoons butter

grated zest and freshly squeezed juice of 3 lemons

100 g/½ cup caster/white sugar

3 large egg yolks

Filling

6 sheets leaf gelatine

300 g/1⅓ cups cream cheese

250 g/generous 1 cup mascarpone cheese

100 g/½ cup caster/white sugar

4 balls stem ginger, finely chopped, plus 60 ml/¼ cup of the syrup

250 ml/1 cup double/heavy cream

a 23-cm/9-in. round springform cake pan, greased and lined with baking parchment

Serves 12

Begin by preparing the lemon curd topping. Put the butter, lemon juice and sugar in a heatproof bowl set over a pan of simmering water. Whisk until the sugar has dissolved, then remove from the heat and set aside to cool slightly. Whisk in the egg yolks and lemon zest, then return the bowl to the pan over the water and stir continuously until the curd thickens. Leave to cool completely.

For the crumb case, crush the Ginger Cookies to fine crumbs in a food processor. Transfer the crumbs to a mixing bowl and stir in the melted butter. Press the buttery crumbs into the base and sides of the prepared cake pan firmly, using the back of a spoon. You need the crumbs to come up about 3–4 cm/1½ in. high.

To make the filling, soak the gelatine leaves in water until they are soft. In a large mixing bowl, whisk together the cream cheese, mascarpone and sugar until light and creamy, then beat in the chopped ginger pieces. Put the ginger syrup and 120 ml/½ cup water in a heatproof bowl set over a pan of simmering water and heat gently. Squeeze the water out of the gelatine leaves and add them to the warm ginger syrup, stirring until the gelatine dissolves. Carefully add the ginger syrup to the cream cheese mixture, passing it through a sieve/strainer as you go to remove any undissolved gelatine pieces. Add the double/heavy cream and whisk everything together until the mixture is smooth and thick.

Pour the filling into the crumb case and tap it gently so that the mixture is evenly distributed. Chill in the fridge for at least 3 hours before serving with spoonfuls of the lemon curd swirled on top.

Perfect for toasting at breakfast time, lunchtime sandwiches, anytime snacks or using to make croutons and breadcrumbs for inclusion in other gluten-free recipes, these versatile and delicious savoury and sweet breads are simplicity itself to bake.

breads

seeded loaf

110 g/1 cup millet flakes

350 g/2½ cups millet flour

3 teaspoons baking powder

1½ teaspoons salt

450 ml/1¾ cups sparkling mineral water (or beer)

1 tablespoon olive oil

1 teaspoon apple cider vinegar

2 tablespoons seeds of your choosing (pumpkin, sesame and sunflower work well)

a 23 x 12 cm/9 x 4¾ in. loaf pan

Makes 1 loaf

Croutons

3 slices Seeded Loaf (see recipe above)

3 tablespoons olive oil

¼ teaspoon salt (or tamari)

1 teaspoon dried herbs of your choosing

a 23 x 30 cm/ 9 x 12 in. baking pan, well-oiled

Serves 3

This lovely loaf is both gluten-free and yeast-free, so you don't need to knead it or wait for it to rise, and it stays fresh for a couple of days! It's also fantastic for making crunchy croutons to add to soups and salads.

Preheat the oven to 220°C (425°F) Gas 7.

Stir together the millet flakes, flour, baking powder and salt in a bowl until well mixed. In a separate bowl, whisk together the sparkling water (or beer) with the olive oil. Pour this into the dry ingredients, mixing vigorously with a spatula until you get a medium-thick batter.

In order to get a nicely shaped loaf, cut a sheet of baking parchment to fit inside the loaf pan without any creases. Sprinkle with 1 tablespoon of the seeds. Pour the dough into the pan and top with the remaining seeds. Bake in the preheated oven, reduced to 200°C (400°F) Gas 6 for 1 hour.

Remove from the oven and tip the bread out of the pan, peel off the paper and let cool completely on a wire rack. Wrap the bread in a dish towel and store in a cool, dry place for up to 5 days.

Variation

To make croutons, preheat the oven to 180°C (350°F) Gas 4. Cut the bread into small cubes. Mix the other ingredients in a large mixing bowl with 2 tablespoons of water and pour over the bread cubes, making sure that each one is coated. Spread the cubes out on the prepared baking pan and bake in the preheated oven for about 30 minutes, until the croutons turn golden brown and crispy. Check and stir every 5 minutes to ensure that the croutons bake evenly. Don't worry if they are a little soft when removing them from the oven – the croutons will dry out as they cool down.

Soda bread is traditionally from Ireland and is very quick and easy to prepare. It contains no yeast as the recipe uses bicarbonate of/baking soda to make it rise. It is great to serve with soups and casseroles. Cutting the cross on top of the loaf is important as it allows it to cook all the way through.

soda bread

Preheat the oven to 180°C (350°F) Gas 4.

Put the bread and oat flours in a large mixing bowl and add the bicarbonate of/baking soda and the salt. Add the buttermilk and milk and mix to form a soft dough. If it is too sticky, add a little more flour but don't overwork the dough – as there is no yeast, you need to keep the mixture as light as possible.

Form the dough into a round mound, about 4 cm/1½ in. high and 20 cm/8 in. in diameter. Cut a cross on the top of the loaf with a sharp knife and dust the top with a little extra flour. Put the loaf on the prepared baking sheet and bake in the preheated oven for 45–55 minutes, until the bread is crusty on top and makes a hollow sound when tapped.

The bread is best eaten on the day you make it, but can be reheated in the oven the following day.

Note

Oat flour is available in health food shops and online, but if you cannot find it, substitute with gluten-free plain/all-purpose flour.

350 g/2¾ cups gluten-free strong brown bread flour, plus extra for dusting

200 g/1½ cups gluten-free oat flour (see Note)

1 teaspoon bicarbonate of soda/baking soda

1 teaspoon salt

500 g/2 cups buttermilk

80 ml/⅓ cup milk

a baking sheet, greased

Makes 1 loaf

150 ml/⅔ cup warm milk

1 tablespoon fast-action dried yeast

1 tablespoon caster/granulated sugar

300 g/2⅓ cups gluten-free strong white bread flour

1 teaspoon baking powder

1 teaspoon xanthan gum

1 teaspoon salt

1 egg, beaten

125 ml/½ cup set plain yogurt

1 tablespoon ghee (clarified butter), melted and cooled, plus extra for brushing

scant 1 tablespoon black onion seeds

yellow cornflour/fine cornmeal, for dusting

2 large baking sheets, greased

Makes 6

These delicious Indian breads are a perfect accompaniment to curries and other spiced dishes. You can add any flavourings you like in place of the black onion seeds, such as a little garlic or finely chopped coriander/cilantro.

naan bread

Put the warm milk, yeast and sugar in a jug/pitcher and leave in a warm place for about 10 minutes until a thick foam has formed on top of the liquid.

Sift the flour, baking powder and xanthan gum into a large mixing bowl. Add the salt, egg, yogurt, melted ghee and onion seeds and the yeast mixture and mix well with a wooden spoon until everything is incorporated and you have a soft dough. Divide the dough into 6 portions.

Dust a clean surface generously with yellow cornflour/cornmeal and roll out each portion of dough into an oval shape, dusting the rolling pin with yellow cornflour/cornmeal, too, so that the bread does not stick. Place the rolled-out naan breads onto the prepared baking sheets and leave in a warm place for about 45 minutes–1 hour until the naan have risen and are slightly puffy.

Preheat the oven to 200°C (400°F) Gas 6 and place the baking sheets inside. Heat the baking sheets for 5 minutes until they are very hot. Carefully place the naan breads on the baking sheets and cook for 4–5 minutes.

Remove the bread from the oven and heat a wok or large frying pan/skillet until very hot. Add the naan breads to the pan, one at a time, and cook for a few minutes on each side until the naan have their classic brown spots. Brush the extra melted ghee over the top of the naan using a pastry brush and serve straight away.

quick cornbread

260 g/1⅔ cups polenta/cornmeal

75 g/scant ⅔ cup gluten-free plain/all-purpose flour

1½ teaspoons baking powder

1 teaspoon salt

1 teaspoon white sugar

100 g/scant ½ cup light brown sugar

1 egg

360 ml/1⅓ cups milk

5 tablespoons vegetable oil

1 roasted red (bell) pepper, diced

kernels from 1 cooked corn cob or 180 g/⅔ cup canned or frozen sweetcorn kernels

1 fresh red chilli/chile, finely diced

2 teaspoons dried chilli/hot red pepper flakes

1½ tablespoons fresh parsley, roughly chopped

30 g/1 oz. feta or goat's cheese, crumbled

butter or cream cheese, to serve (optional)

a medium-sized loaf pan, greased and lined with baking parchment

Makes 1 loaf

There are lots of different ways to make cornbread and many different ingredients you can add to it. Feel free to experiment, as this recipe works just as well plain or made with different herbs and cheeses, and goes really well with scrambled eggs.

Preheat the oven to 200°C (400°F) Gas 6.

Put the polenta/cornmeal, flour, baking powder, salt and sugars in a large mixing bowl and stir to combine. Put the egg, milk and oil in a separate mixing bowl and whisk lightly. Make a well in the centre of the dry ingredients and pour in the egg mixture. Stir well to combine. Then add the red (bell) pepper, sweetcorn, chilli/chile, dried chilli/hot red pepper flakes, parsley and cheese and mix well.

Pour the mixture into the prepared loaf pan and bake in the preheated oven for 25–30 minutes, until a skewer inserted into the middle comes out clean.

Cut into slices and serve as they are, or spread with butter or cream cheese, if liked.

250 g/2 cups gluten-free
self-raising/rising flour, plus
3 teaspoons baking powder
(or 250 g/2 scant cups gluten-free
plain/all-purpose flour, plus
4 teaspoons baking powder
and ½ teaspoon xanthan gum)

3 eggs, beaten

50 g/3½ tablespoons butter,
melted and cooled

280 ml/1 cup plus 2 tablespoons
buttermilk

60 g/generous ½ cup grated
Gruyère cheese

60 g/generous ½ cup grated
Cheddar cheese

1 tablespoon black onion seeds

1 tablespoon freshly snipped
chives

3 tablespoons finely grated
Parmesan cheese

a 23-cm/9-in. springform cake
pan, greased and lined

Makes 1 loaf

Making gluten-free bread dough is very different from making regular bread dough. The steps to creating this tasty loaf couldn't be simpler, as it requires no kneading and no proving. This bread keeps well if stored in an airtight container and is delicious for sandwiches. You can also substitute other flavours in place of the cheese and onion seeds if you prefer.

crusty cheese and onion bread

Preheat the oven to 180°C (350°F) Gas 4.

Sift the flour and baking powder into a large mixing bowl. Add the eggs, melted butter and buttermilk. Fold in the Gruyère and Cheddar cheeses together with the onion seeds and chives, until everything is mixed together well.

Spoon the mixture into the prepared cake pan – the mixture will be quite sticky and resemble cake batter rather than traditional bread dough.

Sprinkle the Parmesan over the top and bake in the preheated oven for 40–50 minutes, until the top of the loaf is golden and springs back to your touch. Let cool in the pan for about 5 minutes before turning out onto a wire rack to cool completely.

This bread will keep for up to 3 days if stored in an airtight container.

walnut and raisin focaccia

100 g/⅔ cup (dark) raisins

125 ml/½ cup Sherry

7 g/1 envelope fast-action dried yeast

1 tablespoon caster/granulated sugar

80 ml/⅓ cup warm water

450 g/3½ cups gluten-free strong white bread flour

250 ml/1 cup warm milk

2 eggs, beaten

1 teaspoon balsamic vinegar

1 teaspoon salt

100 g/⅔ cup walnut halves

a few sprigs of fresh rosemary

olive oil, for drizzling

coarse sea salt

a 33 x 23-cm/13 x 9-in shallow-sided baking pan, greased with olive oil

Makes 1 large loaf

This is a delicious autumnal focaccia bread, topped with crunchy nuts and plump, juicy raisins that have been soaked in Sherry. It makes a great accompaniment to all sorts of soups and salads, or can be enjoyed on its own as a snack. It is best served warm on the day it is made.

Begin by soaking the raisins in the sherry for about 3 hours until the fruit has plumped up.

Put the yeast, sugar and warm water in a jug/pitcher and leave in a warm place for about 10 minutes until a thick foam forms on top of the liquid.

Sift the flour into a large mixing bowl and add the yeast mixture, warm milk, eggs, vinegar and salt and whisk together until everything is incorporated. Spoon the mixture into the baking pan, cover with a damp dish towel and leave in a warm place for 1 hour until the dough has doubled in size and risen.

Preheat the oven to 190°C (375°F) Gas 5.

Drain the raisins and sprinkle them over the dough, along with the walnuts. Poke small sprigs of rosemary into the dough at regular intervals. Drizzle the loaf generously with olive oil and sprinkle with sea salt. Bake in the preheated oven for 35–40 minutes until the bread springs back to the touch and has a crusty top. Serve warm or cold.

2 ripe bananas

115 g/1 stick butter, softened

115 g/½ cup plus 1 tablespoon caster/granulated sugar

2 large eggs

115 g/1 cup gluten-free self-raising/rising flour (or 115 g/1 scant cup gluten-free plain/all-purpose flour, plus 1 teaspoon baking powder and ¼ teaspoon xanthan gum)

3 tablespoons buttermilk

2 teaspoons ground cinnamon

1 teaspoon ground mixed spice/apple pie spice

100 g/1 cup brazil nuts, coarsely chopped

Salted caramel glaze

15 g/1 tablespoon butter

1 tablespoon light soft brown sugar

1 tablespoon golden/light corn syrup

¼ teaspoon fine salt

2 x 450-g/1-lb. loaf pans, greased and lined with baking parchment

Makes 2 loaf cakes

Banana bread is perennially popular, especially when served warm from the oven, cut in thick slices and generously spread with butter. The addition of brazil nuts here gives this loaf cake a lovely texture, but you can substitute any nuts you prefer – pistachios or hazelnuts both work well.

banana and brazil nut loaf

Preheat the oven to 180°C (350°F) Gas 4.

Put the bananas in a bowl and mash with a fork. Put the butter and sugar in a large mixing bowl and whisk until light and creamy. Add the eggs one at a time, whisking after each addition. Add the mashed banana, flour, buttermilk, cinnamon, mixed spice/apple pie spice and brazil nuts and fold in until everything is incorporated.

Divide the batter between the prepared loaf pans and bake in the preheated oven for 25–30 minutes, until the loaves are firm to the touch and a knife inserted in the middle of each cake comes out clean. Remove the loaves from the oven and let cool slightly while you make the glaze.

To make the salted caramel glaze, heat the butter, sugar, syrup and salt in a saucepan or pot set over a medium heat, until the butter has melted and the sugar dissolved. Drizzle the caramel over the warm cakes to glaze, and leave for a few minutes before turning out onto a wire rack to cool.

These loaves will keep for up to 3 days if stored in an airtight container. They also freeze very well, so if you don't need both, you can freeze one for up to 2 months.

index

picture credits

Martin Brigdale
Pages 90–97

Peter Cassidy
Pages 25, 52, 53, 66, 69, 98

Jonathan Gregson
Pages 18, 26

Richard Jung
Pages 118

Steve Painter
Page 125

William Reavell
Pages 1–10, 13, 17, 21, 27–35, 38, 41, 42, 46–51, 54–57 62, 63, 77–82, 101–106, 112–117, 126-132, 134–140, endpapers

Kate Whitaker
Pages 12, 14, 22, 58, 65, 76, 84–89, 100, 109, 121, 122

Clare Winfield
Page 37

Polly Wreford
Page 45, 61, 70–75, 110, 111

recipe credits

Jordan Bourke
Broccoli and Chorizo Tart
Chicken Tagine
Chocolate Tart
Fruit and Nut Flapjacks
Pancakes with Fried Bananas
Pear Apple and Pecan Crumble
Polenta Pizza
Porridge
Quinoa with New-season Beans, Peas
  and Asparagus
Root Vegetable Fritters

Chloe Coker and Jane Montgomery
Baked Cheesecakes with Salted Honey
  Walnuts
Corncakes with Spicy Avocado Salsa
Courgette Fritters with Minted Yogurt
Quick Cornbread
Saffron and Pepper Frittata with Roasted
  Garlic Aioli
Vegetable and Lentil Moussaka

Ross Dobson
Black-eyed Bean and Red Pepper Salad with
  Warm Halloumi
Semolina Crumpets
Slow-cooked Pork Belly with Soya Beans
  and Miso
Spanish Bread Salad

Amy Ruth Finegold
Buckwheat Noodles with Pak Choi, Cashews
  and Tamari Sauce
Chocolate Cupcakes with Almond Butter
  Frosting
Quinoa Spaghetti with Chilli Crab
Red Quinoa Chicken and Mushroom Salad
Shaved Broccoli and Buckwheat Salad

Liz Franklin
Olive Oil and Orange Cake

Tonia George
Caramelized Chicory with Black Forest Ham
  and Poached Eggs
Nutty Honey Granola

Dunja Gulin
Creamy Green Soup
Seeded Loaf
Polenta Tarte Flambée
Pure Energy Bars
Seed Falafel

Jenny Linford
Buttermilk Fried Chicken

Uyen Luu
Sweet and Spicy Spareribs

Hannah Miles
Introduction pages 8–11
Banana and Brazil Nut Loaf
Breakfast Muffins
Buckwheat and Cherry Cake
Buttermilk Scones
Caramel Shortbread
Cheese Crackers
Crusty Cheese and Onion Bread
Four Cheese Scones
Ginger Cookies
Italian Puff Canapés
Lasagne
Lemon and Ginger Cheesecake
Naan Bread
Pear and Almond Sponge
Pork Sausage Rolls
Smoked Haddock Scotch Eggs
Soda Bread
Tomato, Basil and Feta Muffins
Walnut and Raisin Foccacia
White Chocolate and Walnut Brownies

Laura Washburn
Beef and Courgette Gratin
Chicken and Sweet Potato Pot Pie
Meatloaf
Salmon, Broccoli and Potato Gratin
  with Pesto